JOURNEYMEN

BOXING'S TRUE HEROES

JOHN MUTTER

Dedication:

For every single person who steps foot in the squared circle
and participates in the brutal sport of boxing to entertain us
vampiric fans, this is for you.

Contents

PROLOGUE

What is a 'journeyman' boxer? When we present this query to *Google*, the generic definitions disgorged in response include innumerable derogatory terms interpreted somewhat languidly.

'Paid to lose'; 'not quite good enough to be a champion or contender'; 'reliable but not outstanding'. These are but a minute assemblage of ungracious phrases doing a colossal disservice to the population of journeymen fighting in Britain today.

Indeed, times change and the descriptions us humans give to things transpose over time, too. But to the unwitting and ignorant onlookers of boxing, the title 'journeyman' continues to harbour negative connotations.

It cannot aid and abet one in endeavouring to shed an optimistic light on the meaning, particularly when journeymen themselves proclaim, 'I sold my soul to the flesh trade. I paraded isolated muscles controlled by an isolated mind. Promoters and managers are the farmers, and we are the cattle', as Michael Murray, former boxer, and author of *The Journeyman*, once did.

For me, however, 'journeyman' is a genderless expression, encompassing efficacious overtones contrary to popular and historical belief.

Nate Campbell, former *International Boxing Federation* (*IBF*) and *World Boxing Organisation* (*WBO*) Lightweight (135 lb) Champion of the World, heaps praise on the journeyman, declaring, 'Journeymen are the foundation of boxing... Journeymen make boxing. Without journeymen you don't get Miguel Cotto or Nate Campbell, or Joan Guzmán... You give me ten guys who are journeymen and I'll give you fifteen or twenty guys that they [the journeymen] made world champions.'

Away from the glitz, glamour, and riches of the Mayweathers, Joshuas, and Furys, the journeymen introduced in this book represent a growing fragment of the 1,100 licensed professional boxers actively operating in the UK at the time of writing, many of whom have little or no support in not only gaining financial stability from the sport, but also in maintaining their very health and wellbeing.

I'll make no attempt at omitting the exhausted hyperbole so often used in pugilistic debate; conversely, many of boxing's clichés will prove to be functional tools in conveying the full meaning in the pages ahead.

Figuring out this book truly has felt akin to how I imagine it would be to go 12 rounds with a well-seasoned professional championship-level boxer, fighting him in his own town with the referee and judges on his side... And I'm blindfolded... With my hands tied behind my back... With no cut man present in my corner to fix me up.

The enigma of calculating the optimum distance from which to throw a punch, which punch to throw, from which angle, how hard, at which specific exposed body part, followed up by which move to make in order to circumvent a returned fistic assault and impending damage, has, in my imagination, presented identical notions to piecing together the splinters of ideas into one singular, cohesive narrative to form this publication.

Whilst Covid-19 brought about global mania, disrupting millions of lives and heaping misery, uncertainty, and fear upon everyday folk like you and I, it was in the midst of this chaos that my obsession with boxing really battered me into a neutral corner and unleashed a barrage of hooks, crosses, and uppercuts on me, unrelenting, and terminating any chance I ever had of disconnecting from the sport.

Like much of the British population, Covid-19's forceful partitioning of social and familiar groups piloted me towards increased utilisation of social media, be it through necessity to lash together the ruptured bridges of communication, or simply as a way of satiating the incessant boredom of lockdown.

I began to use *Twitter* (now *X*) and *Instagram* to channel my hobbies and interests, hoping to 'meet' and converse with new people about similar passions, and optimistically impel the Virus' impending doom to the back of my mind, if only for a short while at a time.

Without even fully understanding what the word 'journeyman' meant, I elected to name my social media account 'Journeyman's Archives', where it was me who was supposed to be the 'journeyman' and my 'archives' were merely a feeble attempt at becoming some form of important text in all-things-boxing-related discussions online.

I set about reviewing and deliberating over many historical bouts; from Jack Johnson vs Stanley Ketchel; Sugar Ray Leonard vs Roberto Durán; Cassius Clay vs Henry Cooper; Marco Antonio Barrera vs Erik Morales; Joe Calzaghe vs Jeff Lacy; Tony Canzoneri vs Jack Berg; to the lesser-known clashes which have just as much entitlement to adorn the pages of pugilistic tomes on bygone days.

I was eagerly devouring publications such as *The Ring* and *Boxing News* within the first few hours of their respective regular releases, whilst simultaneously masticating all manner of biographical material, films and documentaries related to the sport.

I unexpectedly and inadvertently unearthed a behaviour and newly developed sentiment within myself: rather than, as the pattern of my life had led me to believe, support and cheer for the participant on the winning side, I found myself not only sympathising with, but championing the losing competitor with intrigue and genuine fascination, wondering *why do you fight on?* The more I acquired an understanding of what a journeyman was and why one would pursue this route within boxing, the greater my affinity with and respect for their craft I procured.

During the apathetic months of Covid-19 I spawned the designs of a book on boxing, and before long this objective morphed into a text specifically studying and appraising journeymen. Still, this wasn't enough to actually provoke me into booting up my *iMac* and laying the foundations of a book concerning these brave men and women so key to the sport of boxing.

Until... Whilst sitting on my sofa on a temperate June afternoon, patio doors hooked open, and an appreciated benign, cooling breeze venturing into my lounge, my son at pre-school, wife at work, and daughter asleep in an upstairs bedroom, I was making the most of a peaceful two hours devoid of parenting responsibilities, perusing the journalistic genius of the latest issue of *Boxing News*. And just as if I was the trainer holding my hands out to catch the prodigal boxer who has left every ounce of his existence in the ring following a death-defying, soul-sapping 12-round contest, it fell into my palms willingly: the name Harley Collison. A name which stirred up distant indeterminable memories. One of which I was long unhitched from, and wholly powerless in the task of placing within the context of this magazine and this brutal sport.

Names are far from unique in this day and age, especially within a global population of 8.1 billion human beings striving for individuality, but I had this unrelenting hunch that this Harley Collison was no replica of a Harley Collison I once knew growing up. The Harley Collison who once roamed the same council setting of Pound Road, Pennington, Hampshire, as I did.

I frantically unlocked my *iPhone*, tapped the *Safari* icon and navigated to *Google*, where I typed in 'Harley Collison boxer'. The top result including the information I provided led me to click the link to *boxrec.com* where I was immediately rendered gobsmacked! *The* Harley Collison I had spent a segment of my childhood kicking a football around with, playing 'kerby' (a game where one throws a ball at the opposition's kerb in the hope it will bounce back), and generally chatting about trivial childish subjects, was indeed a professional boxer, at the inception of his career 'punching for pay'!

And this is where we begin, at the launch of a journey where thousands of pounds exit my bank account in exchange for many hours attending small hall shows and arena events, and tonnes of boxing literature dropping through my letterbox over the next couple of years in a never-ending forage for a depth in knowledge where boxing and its contributors are concerned.

The pages and chapters which follow are but a surface scratch on top of the gaping, ever-bleeding contusion of knowledge and intelligence available on journeymen and boxing, where, for the sake of time, six regularly-fighting boxers will represent the other 1,094 (or so) making a living in the same way in Britain.

These six fighters have, in one way or another, imprinted on me and not just *become* an essential part of the story, but *are* the story.

Dale (left/right) w/ boxing legend grandfather Roy Richardson – photos courtesy of Dale Arrowsmith

NAME	Dale Arrowsmith
D.O.B	22nd July 1994
BIRTHPLACE	Stockport, Cheshire
FIGHTS OUT OF	Hyde, Lancashire
DEBUT PRO FIGHT	24th October 2015
FIRST WIN	15th July 2016
FROM DEBUT TO WIN	265 days
FIGHT WEIGHT	Super-welter (154 lb)
PRO RECORD	6-106-4

CHAPTER 1
Dale Arrowsmith

'He was five feet, seven inches and weighed about ten stone, but he felt like a giant.' Roy Richardson, a 'legend' of the Manchester amateur boxing scene, 'Cut his teeth in the carnival boxing booths of Longford Park... taking on all-comers for money.'

Following the Second World War, and his discharge from the Royal Engineers, Roy Richardson's national service was concluded. He married and emigrated to New Zealand, where his affinity with boxing continued as he began training a new generation of Kiwi fighters at a local club.

Upon his return to the UK in the early 1970s, he immediately started to train at the Steelworks gym in Stockport. Richardson trained several boxers who achieved success at national amateur level and he won an assortment of North-West area titles with a number of his protégés.

Upon the sad loss of Manchester boxing hero Richardson at the age of 88 years, as a result of a long and futile battle with Alzheimer's disease, the Steelworks gym was renamed Roy Richardson's Boxing Academy in honour of his exemplary contribution to the sport, and remains to this day a hive of thudding leather and sweat-sodden floors in Compstall, Stockport; an immortal homage to a boxing stalwart.

Is it any wonder, then, that a love for the glove was passed down through his family to granddaughter, Stacey Copeland, who became the first female British Commonwealth boxing champion, and a grandson whom, to date (31st May 2024), has fought a flummoxing 116 professional ring battles?

****

It was not, as has become common convention in the sport of modern boxing, a problematic upbringing or an anguished exploration for direction, discipline, and structure; rather, a predetermined and inexorable bloodline, saturated with pugilism in its DNA, which piloted Dale Arrowsmith in the direction of the fistic game.

One would assume that in the contemporary age of 'over the top' health and safety regulations, a boxer with more than 50 or so bouts on their record would be near impossible to track down, and that hallucinatory records like Len Wickwar's 340-87-42 (wins-losses-draws) would be located only between the long-forgotten years of 1928-1947. In a sense, one would be correct in such an assumption; there are no active boxers in the UK with the staggering sum of 469 professional martial encounters to boast of. There are, on the other hand, a scattering of 'centurions' (boxers with 100 or more bouts on their record) plying their trade today in boxing rings, from Land's End to John O' Groats.

Despite an awe-inspiring tally of six wins, 106 losses, and four draws, with no sign of letting up, Dale admits, 'We're [journeymen] not invincible, we all get stopped at some point!' He adds that his own formidable record has become a challenge unto himself, where he seeks to better his previous most active year of 29 fights, and also works hard to 'get through fights [he] shouldn't be able to.' Put like this the life of a journeyman seems brimming with ebullience and harlequinades, right? Even listening to Dale's buoyant, light-hearted, energetic expression on the other end of the phone has me believing so.

When we dissect a record as numerically stacked as Dale's, we are faced with the consequential reality that 116 fights equates to 473 rounds of boxing; 1,419 minutes of exchanged clobbering; potentially more than 10,000 punches encountered; with the toll of circa 5,000 hours of training for said fights. And this accounts solely for his licensed bouts, excluding much of a childhood spent boxing and an extensive amateur career, where the risk of damage to the brain and body has been invariably omnipresent.

Born in Stockport and living and fighting out of Hyde, Dale has remained both geographically and metaphysically rooted to his grandfather's boxing foundations in the North-West, an organism sown by the late Roy Richardson which he was not only lucky enough to witness grow and shade later generations, but one which continues to flourish today. Incredibly, Roy Richardson's Boxing Academy remains in the family, with Dale and his brother-manager Louie at the helm.

Interestingly, Louie preceded Dale when it comes to boxing, finding success in the Amateur Boxing Association championships (ABAs); the latter initially pursuing the team-oriented sport of football. It was only a matter of time, however, before Dale's fighting gene and prolonged exposure to his grandfather's boxing anecdotes marshalled him, at age nine, through the ropes and onto the canvas of a boxing ring.

Dale brushes off with arbitrary indifference an amateur career which saw him compete 58 times; no mean feat at such a tender age. To have participated in such a great number of bouts would allude to more than just enjoyment of the sport, and even a steady honing of the craft. Lesser-experienced boxers have gone on to become world champions: Hasim Rahman had just seven amateur bouts, George Foreman had 18, James Toney fought 36, and Rocky Marciano's unlicensed numbers are reported to have been thin. All achieved the highest honours within the combative sphere of boxing,

Dale's amateur vocation, guided by the more-than-apt wisdom of his grandfather, took him all over the world; from Poland to Sweden; Denmark to Cuba, slowly building a wealth of knowledge and adroitness in boxing.

At the age of 21, in October 2015, Dale was equipped and primed to launch his professional boxing career, under the watchful eye of trainer Joe Pennington, but his plans were scuppered at the very first hurdle; an overlooked obstacle in the shape of Youssef al-Hamidi. Dale's intentions when turning over (going pro) were to enter the 'game' as a prospect (a boxer who sets out to build a winning record and win titles), however, al-Hamidi had other ideas, purloining a closely-contested four-round points decision (38-39).

Debut defeat to fellow journeyman al-Hamidi in front of Dale's own fans left him scarlet-cheeked and slack-jawed, procrastinating over the most logical ensuing move. Having diligently promoted the event and sold bundles of tickets, as is customary for the 'home' prospect, a victory, though never guaranteed, was prophesied for Dale.

Unaware of al-Hamidi's aptitude (having beaten the likes of Anthony Crolla early in the Liverpudlian's career), and carrying a losing record, it is fair to attend to the fact that Dale may have underestimated his debut opponent. Having sold 90 tickets for the fight, and paid the 'house' (venue and event organiser), promoter, and Dale's manager, he came away with just £400; a meagre sum when one considers not only the time spent preparing for his debut, but the risk that being punched in the head poses to his very life. 'All that effort for this!', Dale declares.

In the wake of this loss, rather than allowing his boxing aspirations to sink to the bottom of the ocean, Dale took a call from manager Joe Pennington. Pennington informed him that due to losing his very first fight, a lot of other boxers wanted to fight him. He was quickly offered a guaranteed £1,500 to take up the 'away' corner mantle at York Hall, London, the following week, with no obligation to endure the pain-staking process of flogging tickets, and the prospect of walking away from the fight with far heavier pockets. The decision was forged instantly; Dale was to 'hit the road' as a journeyman, relinquishing his dreams of silverware in exchange for fast, hard cash.

He shares with me just how challenging being a travelling fighter can be, declaring that it is not as facile as just turning up, losing, and returning home with stacks of paper bearing royal images. He can recount numerous occasions where young fighters he has trained have seen his lifestyle 'through a keyhole'; fighting regularly for wads of money, and believing they can imitate this with ease and get rich quickly, but after two or three successive defeats they are downtrodden and abandon the sport altogether. Dale exhorts any boxer considering the road a journeyman tramps to be mentally prepared and resilient enough to subsist in this capacity of the sport. It is not only psychological preparedness that a journeyman must be armed with, Dale assures me, but skill and boxing competency also. Staying safe in the ring is critical if an away fighter is to continue to provide their services all year-round.

Dale tells me that the defining factor which sunders a journeyman from a prospect who loses, and quits, is pride. Being able to swallow one's honour and accept that losing is precisely why they earn the money they do so regularly is the only way to succeed. He remarks that there is only one thing which hurts his pride, and that is 'being stopped' (counted out or halted by the referee before the scheduled end of a fight).

'It's not all bright lights and big arenas', Dale tells me when challenging a common misconception amongst aspiring boxers. That said, a fantasy was realised for Dale early in his professional career, and one which he could never have envisaged, not even in the demented, bewildering state of a fever dream. Dale's local hero Ricky Hatton was in the process of artfully dismantling and dethroning long-reigning super-lightweight (140 lb) champion Kostya Tszyu on the eve of 4th June 2005, at the Manchester Arena. Dale watched on in awe, fancifully imagining himself surrounded by a throng of thousands of spectators, whilst gallantly battling it out in the same ring, under the same lights, in that very arena. Fast-forward to April 2018 and Dale's unlikely vision became materiality as he competed in a points loss to Ryan Oliver at the Manchester Arena, a dream come true enough for the Hyde leather-wielder. Jump another four years and Dale was not only fighting again at the Manchester Arena, but was doing so on the undercard of his hero; the Ricky Hatton versus Marco Antonio Barrera show on 12th November 2022, being gifted the privilege of a lifetime in sharing a changing room with the legendary Mexican fighter.

On account of Dale confessing that he 'probably wouldn't have reached British level [as a boxer]' had he pursued the grind of a prospect's career, it is no wonder why he excitedly recollects his encounter with Barrera, chuckling, 'I would never have got to do that [if he wasn't a journeyman]!' Dale's brushing of shoulders with the likes of Hatton and Barrera, however, are more than just glancing claims to fame, as not only does he train at the Manchester legend's boxing gym several times a week, but Hatton's son Campbell, now a professional prospect himself, fought his entire amateur career out of Roy Richardson's Boxing Academy; the gym handled by the Arrowsmith siblings.

Reflecting on his debut thwarting at the hands of Youssef al-Hamidi, Dale pledges respect and forgiveness towards his vanquisher, revealing, 'He's a lovely, lovely guy… He always apologises for beating me on my debut!' He reveals that at any point following a number of consecutive losses, the British Boxing Board of Control (BBBofC) can exercise its right to review and sequester a fighter's license, based on how at risk they perceive said boxer to be. In Dale's opening professional bout with al-Hamidi, this very situation loomed over the Syrian journeyman, like an inky black storm cloud waiting to unleash its deluge and wash away his career. 'I needed a win', al-Hamidi apologetically discloses to Dale.

A boxer's, particularly a journeyman's, career is permeated by such warnings. If a fighter happens to lose 'too many' off the bounce, they will find themselves 'on report', whereby their every move is scrutinised; weight, performance, attitude; and if even the slightest thing is amiss in the Board's eyes, the boxer's license to fight can be revoked indefinitely. Under the same ruling, a stoppage defeat, be it a referee's intervention or a ten-count (product of a knock down), can render a boxer suspended from any ring action for a minimum of 28 days; a time frame exceptionally crippling to the livelihood of journeymen like Dale, who relies on the steady income provided by fighting several times per month. The fragility of maintaining this consistent influx of money, and potential for it to cease at any given moment, Dale says, is why journeymen especially must 'be sensible' with their earnings; something he himself has managed to do, purchasing several properties to secure his future financial wellbeing, and setting aside money to cover any enforced breaks from the sport.

Being a journeyman is not without opportunities, nevertheless, as Dale became eligible for a Central Area title shot against Jack McGann in 2023; a chance he attributes to having built a strong relationship with BBBofC official Les Potts, a man, Dale proclaims, 'does a lot for journeymen [in Britain].' A journeyman's losing record does not permanently incapacitate them where title shots are concerned, I'm assured. If Dale so desired he could request an area title match 'tomorrow', where the primary criteria would most likely be for him to 'pick up a couple of wins.' He warns that there would, however, be dire consequences for harbouring such ambitions. If Dale suddenly 'starts battering' his opposition, then 'nobody would touch [him].' He would very quickly find that his crack at winning a belt in boxing would come conjoined to an indeterminate cavity in his fight calendar, alongside depleted incoming capital.

'What's more important to you?', I ask Dale, 'The opportunity for an area title, or regular income?' 'It's my career, I've got a little girl, and I've got a mortgage to pay', he answers. 'What's the point in going for a title and stopping my phone ringing?', he questions rhetorically.

Where ring successes such as titles and coveted laurels are not something Dale seeks to accomplish, the odd victory is not of complete bewilderment to him. As was to be proved, by accident Dale adds, when he achieved his first professional win against Alan Ratibb in July 2016.

In Dale's corner that night in Norwich was Joe Pennington, who advised his boxer to 'just hit [Ratibb] with the odd pot shot to let him know you're there.' Ratibb came out for the second stanza and swung a telegraphed left hook towards

Dale's head, and the Hyde man, following his second's instructions, ducked and poked out a 'little' right uppercut. The result: Ratibb flat on his face, with referee Bob Williams waving his arms wildly to signal the premature conclusion of a scheduled four-rounder, and Dale the unintentional victor via second round technical knockout (TKO).

Dale reminisces about his inadvertent TKO of Ratibb with a chuckle, but accepts the severity of even one win in such fashion on his own record. Dale was not offered any bouts for almost two months following his Ratibb hiccup; an unusually long interruption to a journeyman's busy schedule.

In order to secure a fight, Dale felt compelled to re-enter the squared circle as the home fighter, sharing ticket-selling duties with opponent Steven Backhouse, who went on to stop Dale for the first time ever in the opening round. Backhouse was desperately searching for a win to repair the damage of a prior loss and rejuvenate his own career, whereas Dale could argue that a loss for himself was the perfect remedy for removing any perceived risk he posed to others, and getting him back into paid, regular work. Ironically, Dale did not set out to lose intentionally to Backhouse, but the Salford-born Mancunian just 'absolutely splattered' Dale.

I speak at length with him about the current state of refereeing and judging in professional boxing, and he expresses flustered frustration at how, although he is well aware that he does not win many fights, he is adamant he frequently wins a round or two in many of the lopsided scores that he is subjected to. He longs for a little more respect to be shown to journeymen in the form of being accredited with a few more winning rounds. Dale believes that in constantly being on the receiving end of shut-out losses (winning no rounds), is a disservice to the loyalty and commitment to the sport by boxers like himself. The result; win, loss, or draw, means nothing to Dale, but a ten-point round where it is deserved here and there would not go amiss.

I struggle to think of any profession out there which is as mentally and physically demanding, and as overtly hazardous as boxing, even more-so *journeyman* boxing. How many jobs are there where you can turn up for work knowing in advance the possibility of leaving on a stretcher, or worse, in a wooden box, is of considerable likelihood? Landmine extraction, perhaps? Snake venom milking? Ice road trucking? The crux of it is, probably, few.

For Dale, a man with an affinity for boxing pumping through his veins, it is facile to envision him in his grandfather's image, passing down invaluable wisdom to future generations of journeymen and prospects alike, stamping his own unique legacy into the annals of the gloved game. It is fair to say that his second's and manager's license will both be as dog-eared through usage as a pilot's passport.

I sign off with one closing question for Dale: 'So what is a journeyman?'

'We are paid to lose, it's as simple as that. We are the gate-keepers. If you are a good prospect, you should be beating me or getting me out of there!'

Journeymen, like Dale, are the puzzles for dissectologists; there to separate the wheat from the chaff; pan the gold from the clay', and propel the stars into the stratosphere.

Matt, hand raised in rare victory – photo courtesy of Michael Ault

NAME	Matt Hall
D.O.B	22nd March 1992
BIRTHPLACE	Wordsley, West Midlands
FIGHTS OUT OF	Brierley Hill, West Mids.
DEBUT PRO FIGHT	1st September 2017
FIRST WIN	19th October 2019
FROM DEBUT TO WIN	778 days
FIGHT WEIGHT	Super-welter (154 lb)
PRO RECORD	3-119-3

CHAPTER 2
Matt Hall

'They've all got two hands and a head... I'll box anybody!'

For Brierley Hill self-avowed journeyman Matt Hall, undergoing a rigorous training camp in preparation for a specific fighter and style is simply not on the super-welter's agenda. Nor is stepping through the ropes and onto the canvas with a game plan to harm his opponent and ultimately feel the firm grip of the referee's fingers around his gloved wrist as his hand is raised in a concluding symbol of conquest.

The 778-day intermission joining Matt's paid launch bout with then unbeaten 3-0-0 Tom Young, and his opening victory against Terry Maughan, a run-back of their previous draw in March 2019, felt less a period of waiting to him than it would have to many of today's hopeful champions crossing the threshold of professional boxing. Matt never began his journey as a pro pugilist with the vision of achieving stardom or holding titles, rather, from his genesis in the sport he espoused the away corner mantle with one tunnel-visioned, elementary mission: to financially provide for his wife and young child (to become children).

Native of the Black Country, Matt's life is stapled to the West Midlands, where he is a proud husband of a decade to Laura, and father to three children; Callum, Joseph, and Amelia. His own childhood 'wasn't a life of luxuries', nevertheless, he opines that by no account did he ever suffer deprivation of anything, essential or desired. He confesses that his unexceptional upbringing and pining for his own offspring to experience fulfilment in a way he did not, is the rationale supporting his election to fight for more than just nobbins.

At the time Matt turned over, he and Laura only had little Callum, and sought to impart upon him a 'better life'; a trove bursting with beatific memories and a want for nothing. When Joseph and Amelia came along, Matt's motivation to accord his children a 'good start to life' was indestructible, and he recognised with limitless appreciation that boxing was to manifest that very platform.

Disparate to your typical prospective champion boxer, Matt's complicity in the gloved sport is not deep-rooted or connected to a profound impetus, instead, he virtually unearthed boxing inadvertently. His only real experience in a gym was for the purpose of lifting weights, and it was not until a good friend of his signed up for a charity boxing event, and in order to propel the fund-raising exhibition towards success, Matt donated his fists to the cause. He recollects that he 'just took to it from there' where boxing was concerned. Matt conveys confounded gaiety in his embroilment in contributing to charitable boxing, organising and fighting on his own show shortly after, finding 'a love for the sport.'

Matt's foot was well and truly through the ropes by this point, with him taking part in a handful of 'white collar' and unlicensed bouts, catapulting him into a form of title shot at this level, despite his relative inexperience. He found himself hurled in against Kevin McCauley, an accomplished fighter of more than 200 bouts to boot, and a man who went on to retire with 251 professional ring battles to his name. Matt characterises himself as having been 'green' at this early stage, disclosing that he was oblivious to who McCauley even was, or of his opponent's capabilities.

Yet, in the wake of Matt's trading of leather with McCauley, his affable adversary encouraged him to start earning money from fighting, sharing that he believed Matt was 'tough' and would 'do well on the road as a journeyman.' A notion Matt says he initially 'laughed off.' McCauley persisted and entreated Matt to attend some small hall boxing shows with him, so as to 'get a feel' for how away fighters function, and Matt instantly delighted in the entire conglomeration of journeyman boxing. He apprises that he latched on to the knowledge, then and there, that he did not want to pursue the path of a 'prospect' or 'home' fighter. Matt shares that he did, however, only enter into boxing professionally as a short-term career, with the intention of solely earning enough money to front a deposit on a house, which he approximated to be circa ten to 15 fights. It is incontestable that the bug clung on and Matt's passion for pugilism, as he puts it, 'snowballed.'

His seamless remoulding from 'man on the street' to professional boxer gives the impression of 'money for jam', but Matt warns us not to be hoodwinked into believing all is rose-coloured. He expounds his constant melee with making the 154 lb super-welterweight limit, which is essential to both his performance and wellbeing in the ring, owing to the fact that his stability would greatly decay if pitched against fighters in heavier divisions. He insists that it is the speed of the young, flashy, keen prospects which troubles him more than heavy power shots from a 'clubber', but as with any typical step up in weight, the power exuded by punches from men at super-middleweight (168 lb) and above, becomes exponentially more bothersome and minacious for a compact boxer like Matt.

Reminiscing about his debut defeat to Tom Young, Matt expresses a blithe indifference to the result, inferring that in his position it is more prudent to lose than win. He attributes this concept to the certitude that when he has, on rare occasions albeit, been victorious in the squared circle, his phone has 'stopped ringing' with offers of bouts, and therefore income. He jests that wins for journeymen are 'like buses… You wait around all day for one, then two come along!' As was the case when he triumphed in his rematch with Terry Maughan in October 2019. Matt immediately, and unintentionally, followed up this success with his conquest of Carl Chadwick a mere seven days later.

Matt gallantly promulgates that his return bout, and subsequent prevailing over Maughan, 'meant a lot' to him. His first contest with Maughan was adjudged to have been a tie, despite Maughan requiring stitches and appearing to have been thoroughly beaten. Matt tells me he always carries the expectation to lose his fights, but that 'if after feeling [his opponent] out in the first round, they are there for the taking', he will 'go for it.' He believed he had done enough to clinch his first ever professional victory, but referee Chris Dean had other ideas. The draw had little impact on Matt, but what followed would ultimately shape his performance when he met Maughan seven months later.

His world was sent spinning off course with the meteoric news that his mother had been diagnosed with cancer, and after a short battle, she sadly passed away. Around this time Matt received a phone call beseeching the rematch with Maughan, which he eagerly accepted. He brushes delicately past the emotional topic of his mother's passing, but I sense that the vehemence of this astronomical life event found an outlet channel in the form of Terry Maughan.

Matt describes the opening bell of his second fight with Maughan as being more like the fifth bell; a continuation of their first bout, requiring unarguable settlement. He says that he 'took [the fight] to him from the off', and was faced with a brand new sensation just 15 minutes later: having his gloved hand raised in victory.

Matt illustrates to me how he 'learned the hard way' and, for the first time since turning over ten months prior to this win, and 21 fights later, got to see the 'business side' of boxing. He was obliged to sunder his sentiments from his in-ring performance, because a journeyman who becomes a skilled vanquisher very quickly becomes unemployable. By virtue of winning, Matt, and his journeymen counterparts alike, are viewed as posing too sizeable a threat to a prospect's marketable and profitable unbeaten record.

Nowadays, having been a professional boxer for almost seven years, with 125 bouts' experience, Matt proclaims that not only does he enter into fights with no knowledge of his opponents and their skillsets, he also does not even go into them attempting to win. To 'pinch a round' here and there, perhaps, but routine income is his priority, made possible if he simply continues to raise statistics on prospects' records.

Matt depicts his own boxing skills as 'minimal', intimating that his prime concern whilst in the ring is to avoid being cut or stopped by knockout, where his safety takes precedence. He informs me that there have been countless occasions where he has been absolutely certain he has won at least a round or two, but has conversely found himself the recipient of a shut-out loss. This is a common state of affairs that Matt has learnt to just 'laugh off', being that he gets paid the same amount regardless and that it is 'just the game.' He quips, 'If [bad decisions] happen on major televised shows in front of millions, then it's always going to happen on small hall shows in front of a thousand people with no cameras there!' Corruption, misconduct, and delinquency in professional boxing is another talking point we precipitously avert, but one which I make a cerebral note to revisit at a future time when Matt no longer relies on his boxing license for sustenance.

Matt is eager to impart that the role of a journeyman is not all money-making and straightforward four-rounders. He reveals that whilst most of the country's inhabitants are dead to the world, he is awake at the preposterous time of 04:30 every morning, training to maintain fitness and strength to ensure his availability and reliability to fight around Britain's small hall boxing circuit every weekend. He adds that by offering his face to the gloved knuckles of opponents on such a regular basis, this entails immolating time away from his family and friends, often in the form of him travelling many hundreds of miles for 12 minutes of ring action.

'How do your wife and children feel about you getting in the ring and taking punishment?', I ask. 'They used to worry a lot, but they're okay with it now', he answers, adding that they understand his job and trust that he can keep himself out of harm's way. He shares that his children have displayed interest in boxing, but quickly retorts, 'They'll never step foot in a ring, that'll never happen!' This tells me all I need to know about just how much is at stake with every collision between leather and skull. He interjects, 'I do it so that my kids don't have to.'

'With the knowledge and experience you have now, would you change anything if you could start over?', I ponder. 'Yeah, a hundred per cent', he returns. 'I would box more white collar contests and build a sustainable platform', where amateur pedigree may have provided the opportunity to fight less frequently, for more money, with the added benefits of a sellable and protected winning record, with some title honours sprinkled on top.

Matt enthusiastically tells me that fellow journeyman Jordan Grannum is one of the best away fighters in the country, with the ability to easily win more than 80% of his bouts. He has, in fact, won just 11 of 152 professional fights, or 7% of them. This is disclosure enough as to exactly what kind of deal a journeyman receives, even one with the calibre, skill, and promise of Jordan Grannum. More later on him.

As far as injuries go, Matt jokes that one flick on his nose sets it to streaming blood, leaving him with a face resembling Chuck Wepner, famously nicknamed 'The Bleeder'. This is something he says has little effect on his performance and he has grown accustomed to the taste of his own visceral fluids.

In his bout with Steve McKenna in December 2020, Matt encountered a rare technical knockout defeat. He recalls looping a powerful hook to his foe's cranium, and instantly felt shooting pains up his entire arm, as if lightning had struck his fingertip, frying his bones on its travel through him; the result of a broken and dislocated wrist. This all occurred in the opening seconds of the preliminary round. Matt persevered on adrenaline, boxing through to the fifth round of a scheduled six, before referee Ian John-Lewis waved it off, with Matt still on his feet. He conveys irritation at this premature halt, insisting he was comfortable and safe enough to fight on for the remaining four minutes of the bout. A notion shared by former WBA super-middleweight world champion, and commentator that night, George Groves… 'Another home favourite', Matt concedes.

Unbeaten prospect McKenna had already sent his previous three opponents for early showers, and Matt believes his opponent's knockout record was becoming a unique selling point for promoters, so one more stoppage, in the form of Matt, would only intensify the hype surrounding McKenna. Reading between the lines of Matt's frustration, it could be argued that any excuse to build on McKenna's destructive-looking record was being sought.

With respect to Matt's own statistics and responsibilities as a journeyman, I invite him to cede his personal interpretation of exactly what his role in the spot entails. 'I'm the away fighter, giving the prospect the start to their career, a platform to build from.' He recapitulates that any boxer with a winning record greater than four wins to zero losses should not be fighting a journeyman. A journeyman should not be used, Matt argues, 'to pad an opponent's record', they should be employed to provide experience to a prospect and help to expose any knowledge gaps or weaknesses early in their career, with minimal risk to their status.

Matt concludes, 'Any boxer who has won more than four or five and remains unbeaten should only be taking fifty-fifty fights', so as to reveal those capable of 'making it' in professional boxing.

For a man who has had 125 fights, boxing 520 rounds, putting his very existence on the line for 1,560 minutes in the ring, equivalent to 26 hours of his life, Matt admits to me that he 'can see retirement on the horizon', recognising that his children will only 'be young once.' He aims to bow out from the not-so-sweet-science with his health and senses fully intact.

For now, however, the Brierley Hill prize-fighter needs only a 'date and weight' from his manager Errol Johnson, and he will converge with you between those four roped posts.

Jordan sporting his famous 'It's just business' shorts – photo courtesy of Jordan Grannum

NAME	Jordan Grannum
D.O.B	11th October 1992
BIRTHPLACE	London
FIGHTS OUT OF	Islington, London
DEBUT PRO FIGHT	2nd October 2015
FIRST WIN	2nd October 2015
FROM DEBUT TO WIN	0 days
FIGHT WEIGHT	Middleweight (160 lb)
PRO RECORD	11-135-5

CHAPTER 3
Jordan Grannum

Not branded a 'journeyman' from his inception in the professional code of boxing, the 'Brown Eagle' middleweight enumerated a phenomenal record as an amateur, racking up 26 uninterrupted triumphs, before turning over in October 2015, carrying the weight of the world on his shoulders which customarily comes with being stamped a 'prospect'.

Within the basal seconds of our conversation I am immediately warmed with the sense that here is one of the most humble, self-aware individuals that I have ever had the good fortune of encountering.

For innumerable up-and-coming boxers, and those being touted as 'the next big star', or even to many paying fans of the sport, the word 'journeyman', used to describe a boxer on a 'losing' path and regularly providing opponents with uncomplicated experience, is commonly spouted as a dirty word, piggy-backed with cynicism and reproach.

For Jordan, however, I am forthwith put at ease as he explains that he 'never had a problem with the word "journeyman."' He expresses, 'It's quite a fitting title, you're travelling a lot, you're always on a journey!' His discernment of the differentiating roles within boxing, from amateur to professional, journeyman to prospect, and gatekeeper to champion, signifies his absolute cognizance of not just how to effectively handle his job description, but of exactly who he is.

Born in North Middlesex Hospital, London, Jordan spent the first decade of his childhood in the suburban district of Wood Green in the Haringey borough of England's capital; a North London region famous for its three-day annual amateur boxing tournament, The Haringey Box Cup. Given that he was raised just a ten-minute car journey from The Alexandra Palace, the home of the Box Cup, perhaps he was always destined to make a name for himself within the roped arena.

At around the age of 12 years, Jordan's family re-located five miles south, but an interminable 30-minute drive (for such a short distance) to the neighbouring North London locality of Islington. He intimates that his family life 'wasn't the best', but openly accepts that it also 'definitely wasn't the worst', growing up in a 'full' house with his mother, step-father, and two younger siblings; eight and ten years his junior.

His candour strikes me when he shares that his biological father was in trouble 'a lot' with the police when Jordan was growing up, and was in and out of the family home, enduring periods of absence from his son's life, including stanzas in prison. 'Looking back now', Jordan exclaims, 'That will definitely affect a young kid.'

He remembers one such occasion when the authorities arrived at his house and attempted to gain entry by 'kicking the door down' whilst in pursuit of his father. In the face of this, he says he never had to 'deal with anything crazy' and that he did enjoy a contented family life, never wanting for or in need of anything that the average British child has.

Any adverse experiences that Jordan lived through as a youth have been harnessed and up-cycled into lessons on how to treat his own young family, including his partner and two young children; a three-year-old boy and a two-year-old girl, alongside an 11-year-old boy from his partner's previous relationship.

With a balanced concoction of both earnestness and comedic value, Jordan displays no hesitation in telling me that he 'was like electricity', with school being water. He recalls that he was 'trouble' all the way from reception to year ten, when he finally discarded his fractious relationship with the education system. He adds that he also attended a 'pupil referral unit', a place of alternative education for pupils whom find themselves temporarily excluded from mainstream school, as was the case for him in year seven.

His honesty is laudable, sharing with me that his aberration for school stems from lacking respect, and even care for, authority. Whilst he was not a child whom 'threw chairs around the classroom', he grappled with the inability to follow teachers' orders, and so the educational institution became a place of unceasing despondency for him. Providing the surroundings and role-models were sound, this should have been a time and place which proffered a safe haven in which a child could learn and grow.

This skirmish with command never, however, bled into his adult life. Although he had brushes with the police that many struggling youngsters bear, he intelligibly lives on 'the right side' of the law so as to set an example for his own children, and to make certain that he is always there to provide for them.

External demons were always present throughout Jordan's early life, in the form of local gangs and drug dealers, but he managed to 'steer well clear', ultimately deterred by witnessing first-hand some of his own friends being bequeathed lengthy jail sentences, in addition to his own father's 15-year incarceration. Jordan confesses, 'That's never been a place I want to go!', and has actively seen to it that he never 'puts [himself] on offer' to the justice system.

A familiar theme frequently materialises within boxing, whereby an unsettled childhood results in one attending a boxing gym in search of discipline and order. This, however, was not the case for Jordan. His participation in the sport was a perchance 'tagging-along' with a friend at around the age of 14, saying he 'went along [to the gym] to see what it was all about and hated it.' He pins the liability of his initial disapprobation for the boxing club on the fact that he was smoking cannabis a lot at the time and the exercise made him 'sweat profusely'; a new and uncomfortable sensation.

Just one week later he decided to return to the gym, and inadvertently experienced a radical contrast, falling in love with the gloved combat. His progress from hereon in was on a vertical trajectory, and within a year from first lacing up leather mittens, he had trained exhaustively, acquired peak fitness, eradicated marijuana from his 'diet', and was set to participate in his introductory amateur bout. This credits the Londoner, to date, with 17 years' experience as a pugilist.

Alongside coaches Jerry Mitchell and Bevis Allen of Islington Boxing Club, Jordan was victorious in his first Senior Novice title attempt in 2011, following up with a successive National Amateur Championship conquest in 2012.

Jordan, naturally adept at sports, and once on the books of Arsenal's youth football team, developed into a 'boxer-puncher' throughout his amateur career and was, by all accounts, destined for ceiling-less greatness, just a week before his professional debut telling the Islington Gazette newspaper, 'I think I can be challenging for world titles in four or five years!'

His maiden voyage into the squared circle as a paid professional could not have fared better, seeing his hand raised in a points triumph over William Warburton at the Camden Centre, King's Cross, on 2nd October 2015.

He built on his debut success six months later, with a second professional victory, and consecutive shut-out (40-36) points win, this time against Ali Wyatt at Tolworth Recreation Centre, courtesy of referee Bob Williams.

All was going perfectly until a devastating injury, in the form of a severe leg break, sustained from a motorcycle accident, kept Jordan out of the ring for over a year. He was unable to return to competitive action until June 2017, where his 'prospect' status was dealt a significant blow in the shape of a points defeat to Ryan Brawley over a close (56-58) six-rounder.

Despite, on the face of it, his first loss appearing as a fatal wound at the birth of his professional career, Jordan informs me that even before his full recovery following the motorbike collision, he had already had a myriad of time in which to reflect and construct a scheme for his boxing career. Just two short years after debuting, he not only accepted that he was to transition into a journeyman and leave behind all hopes of future silverware in the sport, but was actually comfortable and content with this arrangement.

He attributes his interchanging mind-set to the fact that when he first turned over as a licensed boxer he sold plenty of tickets and fulfilled his obligation to 'pay the house', whilst making a little money for himself. However, the pressure that coincides with having to regularly sell tickets to friends and family proved to be excessive and unmanageable.

He says it was 'an amazing feeling to make a bit of change' as a pro, but this came to an abrupt halt as, travelling away for his second fight, he only managed to sell around 35 tickets, and after paying his journeyman opposition £1,100 of his £1,300 ticket profits, he was left with the grim realisation that, following sustained efforts to 'hassle' and shift tickets, then self-funding his trip to Tolworth, then putting himself at risk in the ring, he was to walk away with a meagre £200.

In the wake of toiling assiduously for eight long weeks for this fight, the immense loss of potential earnings for Jordan's exertions came hand in hand with a direct depreciation of 'the buzz' he had previously felt in the amateur game.

He explains that the expectations placed upon a prospect boxer include fighting approximately four times per year, but that due to ongoing difficulties with ticket sales, he was forced to cancel several scheduled bouts, which in turn 'murdered' his momentum and ultimately persuaded him to re-assess and re-adapt his role within boxing. Jordan 'took to the road' as a journeyman at this point, earning a considerable amount more money on a regular basis, with the appended bonus of no promotional obligations.

Two elements of his ticket sale conundrum were, initially, the pressure of having those whom know and support him watch him fight, which generated a genuine fear of losing in front of them, and also, not wanting to become a nuisance to people when asking for money periodically, especially when he knew many people were struggling financially in affording the bare essentials, let alone luxuries like event tickets.

Jordan's ultimatum became evidently clear: fight in the away corner, or stop boxing altogether. He discloses with no apparent bitterness whatsoever, 'I'm never going to get that love back that I felt in the amateurs, but this [as an experienced journeyman earning regularly] is the most I've loved it since.'

That he boxes routinely and has established a good reputation and record worthy of continuous offers from promoters and fighters nationwide, results in him not having to look for employment elsewhere. He does, however, carry out personal training and a seafood business (still in its infancy), on the side for pleasure.

There is an abundance of inactive boxers in Britain, many of whom Jordan believes would become more involved in the sport and make a steady living from if they simply 'dropped the ego', and also the attitude where a zero-losses record is so desperately pursued. He says these boxers refuse to 'come to the away corner on account of unjustifiable pride, and laughs the laugh of a man in the know, 'This business is so cruel!'

Jordan swiftly calibrated himself to losing fights, accepting, and even welcoming the fact that he was no longer a prospect, and had ditched the hopes of winning championship belts, participating purely for monetary gain, with one not-so-simple task at hand: not to get stopped! This is an extraordinarily idiosyncratic substitution of thought process from a man whom, as an amateur, boldly proclaimed he 'would rather lose [his] bollocks than a fight!'

He tells me now, 'This is what I want to do... I want to fight, and I want to earn money from it!'

****

As I lean eagerly over the brown-glossed hardwood railing which encompasses the balcony of York Hall's top viewing deck, peering at the black *Goodwin Promotions* canvas, the third bout of the evening comes to a close. Shocki Khan's gloved hand is raised by overseer Mark Bates, signifying victory after a stern six round trading of leather with Jordan Grannum. I can't hide the respect and appreciation I feel in that moment for the losing man. Gracious in defeat, clapping his gloves together in all three surrounding directions of the paying crowd, before offering up a curt nod in the direction of opponent Khan's raucous but loyal followers, Grannum epitomises every good thing about all modern day journeymen, displaying his own respect for the people putting cash in his pocket, but also the value he holds for the sport itself.

****

I enquire of Jordan what he feels and whether, indeed, he feels different on those rare occasions when he is awarded a win. He bluntly but honestly retorts, 'Nothing. Not one bit... Whether their hand gets raised or my hand gets raised, it's no different!'

He expresses that his only concern, arising from the latter nine successes on his record (the first two wins coming at a time when his frame of mind was firmly on titles and championships), was that of rival boxers pulling out or avoiding him altogether, due to the potential risk of him damaging their own records, and ultimately depriving him of his own income.

He goes to the extent of making the intrepid statement that, 'Winning fights really wouldn't make sense', not just where earning money is concerned, but for somebody who 'loves fighting' to suddenly stop being given the opportunity to do so regularly would be injurious to his wellbeing.

I make an attempt to graze the skin of the subject of corruption in boxing; the sort many believe is prevalent in refereeing, judges' results, and even in rumours detailing fighters being told to lose by promoters so as to protect an up-and-comer. Without a hint of hesitation, I am told 'no' and all knowledge of this is denied. Whether this is an automatic mechanism to safeguard his license, and therefore his livelihood, is open to interpretation, but Jordan's adamant tone and rapidity of response gives me no reason to doubt his integrity. He does, on the other hand, inform me that he has had fights where he has 'put the other fighter down in three or four rounds', and still, somehow, despite the expected customary awarding of a 10-8 score for the rounds in question, lost on points. Make of that what you will.

On numerous occasions I have witnessed first-hand 'home' fighters be awarded victories which I, and the spectators in attendance, believed could, and should have gone the other way. More often than not, these results appear to be in favour of preserving a prospect, or debutant's untarnished record, where defeat could scupper all future plans. Jordan graciously attributes much of the leniency of refereeing to the crowd reaction, which, presumably, for a boxer at their home venue will be louder and in favour of its own fighter. I am not categorically convinced by this as there are frequent grumblings from neutral fans of the sport, stamping their feet over unjustifiable outcomes of bouts, particularly around the small hall circuit.

I ask Jordan what changes need to be implemented in order for all aspiring boxers turning over to be given a fair shake. He immediately returns with, 'Scrap the tickets!' He conveys a firm apprehension that this is unlikely to ever be feasible, but alludes to this lone aspect of the professional side of the sport being the constraint under which a prospect is metamorphosed into a journeyman.

An entire small hall boxing show's revenue hinges on the prospects' ticket sales, with up to ten fights, where all away corners must be paid, the 'house' (promoter and venue) demands profits, and managerial personnel take their cuts. Without such income, stemming from comprehensive efforts from the ticket-sellers themselves, the show simply cannot go on.

When one considers the approximate cost of £1,200 just for a boxer's mandatory medicals required to gain a professional license, plus the overwhelming and incessant need to constantly shift tickets, is it any wonder why so many fighters, like Jordan, opt to take the alternative route of a journeyman? He jests that, 'If you could sell a thousand tickets tomorrow, you would see that your medical was already paid for!' Once again, this is damming evidence of money talking, and the sport being more a business for those not taking the punches than a fair competition for the athletes punishing their bodies. An irony adopted by the good-humoured Londoner himself as he sports a pair of red boxing shorts adorned with the quotation 'IT'S JUST BUSINESS'.

The solemnity of the task at hand each time Jordan climbs into the ring is not lost on him. He emphasises that he is 'risking [his] life' week in, week out. Because of this, he has all but perfected the craft of defence, where the majority of gloves making contact with him tend to glance off of his raised arms. But history has taught us that if it isn't an accumulation of blows to the head causing long-term health issues such as

Dementia Pugilistica, then it is that one, flawlessly-executed shot to the 'right' part of the skull which ends the life, then and there on those canvas-laden boards.

Unlike at championship level where competitors are financed to fight twice a year, with lengthy, three-month training camps to prepare for a bout, this luxury is not afforded to the likes of Jordan, who needs to fight regularly in order to keep his kitchen cupboards stocked.

One adverse positive effect of fighting frequently, however, is that his fitness is maintained all year-round, and his weight doesn't fluctuate, therefore keeping his work tools sharp and employment offers flooding in.

Jordan has compiled such a respectable and 'friendly' record that he is often called upon to fight many miles from home, journeying up to 400 miles to destinations such as Glasgow, and this willingness to sacrifice time away from his family ensures his phone continues to ring. He divulges that it does not feel as a big a forfeit as it might for many other journeymen, because boxing is his sole line of work, so he is able to be with his family throughout the week rather than work a second job.

Jordan has the full support from what he describes as a 'boxing family', indicating that when he met his partner he was already boxing regularly, so it was a part of his life pre-embedded and accepted without issues. That, and the fact that his partner's 11-year-old son is the current London Champion, fighting for England title status imminently. The undertone of concern for the health of both son and partner, overshadowed by pride and encouragement, must surely still creep into the corner of Jordan's partner's mind at the very moment the soles of their boots touch the canvas at the start of each fight. Certainly followed by the ceaseless release of held breath, and the ever-welcome relief that the final gong brings, when both escape the sport safely, if only temporarily.

In a sport which brutally crushes the hopes and dreams of most embarking on a quest to bring home belts and trophies, it is remarkably grounding to hear that Jordan's intentions are to remain in boxing long after his body erodes, managing and training future generations of boxers, specifically journeymen, handing down the realities and lessons that he faced the hard way. The 31 year-old, good health permitting, plans to fight on until he is 40. Taking into account the 151 bouts, and nine years spent as a professional in the sport, and assuming the frequency of which he fights does not depreciate, the 16.7 average annual contests would take him to an unfathomable 302 fights! Whilst Jordan's objective is to make it safely to an already-astonishing 200 pro bouts, my mind implodes at the thought of a tri-centurion!

Reflecting back to his first professional battle, Jordan contemplates whether he would live and box under the same circumstances again, or whether he would implement changes. There is a musing break, where he wonders whether the 'out of character' social media push could aid him in mounting a challenge for some form of official honours, or whether, had he understood his role as a journeyman sooner, he could have been 200 fights deep and financially better off. The hypothesis is inconclusive, but Jordan leans towards the journeyman route being the more lucrative, secure option.

I've been a spectator at a handful of Jordan's bouts, and cannot help thinking that a sprinkling of laurels would not have been out of reach, if the might of financial backing was in place and the dog's leash was properly severed...

The 'Brown Eagle', a nickname fashioned unexpectedly for Jordan on a favourite Caribbean takeaway situated in Tottenham, rather than a predatory North American avian, has only ever twice felt his skin touch the mat in over 600 rounds of boxing. This, above all else, verifies just how skilled a journeyman boxer has to be in keeping themselves safe.

For a journeyman who perceives his role in the sport to be a person who is 'always on a journey', and wears his title with resolute fulfilment, long may Jordan's journey continue.

The strains a new fighter faces in selling tickets so that a promoter's pockets can become fatter can often break a boxer. The way I see it is: the choice a boxer makes to become a journeyman, like Jordan did, is like carbon atoms being put under such immense pressure, with no more give available, consequently forming a diamond.

Jake and his son Roman – photo courtesy of Jake Pollard

NAME	Jake Pollard
D.O.B	4th December 1991
BIRTHPLACE	Bradford, West Yorks.
FIGHTS OUT OF	Bridlington, East Yorks.
DEBUT PRO FIGHT	20th October 2018
FIRST WIN	15th July 2023
FROM DEBUT TO WIN	1,729 days
FIGHT WEIGHT	Featherweight (126 lb)
PRO RECORD	1-66-0

CHAPTER 4
Jake Pollard

Born and raised in Bradford, West Yorkshire – 'It's obviously quite a tough place... quite rough... If someone gets shot down the road, it's not a surprise... No-one's shocked or worried.'

Jake Pollard now enjoys life 80 miles east in the neighbouring West Yorkshire city of Bridlington, a place he discerns is a far-cry from the unforgiving setting of his childhood. The violence and threat present in Jake's childhood environment is evident when he divulges, 'If someone got shot on the street here [in Bridlington] you'd never hear the end of it... In Bradford there're shootings and stabbings and fights all the time, it's chaos!'

The Yorkshireman reiterates that every other day one could see a video in the news or on social media of, for example, two cars ramming into one another, where one of the passengers might hop out with a machete, and what follows is the kind of stuff best left in a James Patterson novel.

Spontaneous and unwelcome fights would come easily in Bradford, Jake's old hometown. 'Just being a boxer meant [a fight could happen] without even trying, and that's not what I want to do.' Jake's move to the east coast of the north enabled him to keep his fighting within the skills-based squared circle and off the streets, away from collisions with the law, and worse, a genuine potential risk to life. 'Just driving down the street [in Bradford] you can end up having a confrontation with someone.'

Jake informs me that it wasn't the boxing that succoured his move away from the rugged conurbation of Bradford; the switch of location was a requirement of pursuing his second career as a farrier. 'To get a farrier's apprenticeship, the majority of the time you have to move away.' Jake found work in Hull as a mentee horseshoe smithy, living out of a holiday-style caravan.

The training took a lengthy, gut-busting five years for Jake to gain accreditation and competency in, so his mobile home lifestyle endured in alignment with the time frame of his hammer-and-anvil work.

When Jake's apprenticeship finally came to an end, his parents made the decision to live in Bridlington, also. It was at this time that Jake and his parents traded positions, with the former temporarily making a return to Bradford, but quickly growing 'sick' of his former haunt and opting for permanent residence back in Bridlington. Jake describes Bridlington as 'peaceful' and recounts the perks of living just a five-minute walk from the beach.

Despite the turbulence and disorder of living in Bradford, Jake shares with me that when growing up, his family life was stable. Jake is part of a family of five, with an older brother and younger sister sandwiching him, and, unlike so many families in the present day, parents who stayed together and raised their three children within a happy home.

The family's quarters were situated far enough away from the hustle and bustle of the more crime-stricken areas of Bradford, so his exposure to danger was not always omnipresent. Conversely, Jake states that there was a 'rough estate' near the village he grew up in, and that he'd frequently witness stolen vehicles careering past his home, police in hot pursuit.

Jake considers his youthhood to have been that of a typical '90's child', following his parents' rules with such gestures like 'getting home at night before the streetlights came on.'

Early school life for Jake was settled, with him attending and learning the national curriculum like most regular British children, but he found himself becoming involved in more and more physical altercations as he advanced through 'middle' school. He defends himself unnecessarily to me by noting that he wasn't a 'naughty kid', but because he was a smaller child than the average for his age, he developed the need to stamp his presence in order to prevent him being bullied by his bigger peers, taking a fistic approach to self-preservation.

Jake informs me that these pugnacious proceedings may stem from the teachings of his father. Like all good parents we harbour the desire to see to it that our children are safe and well-protected. Jake confides in me that his father was fostered in care homes throughout his childhood, and so naturally evolved the ability to look after himself, electing to tap any antagonists on the button with the aim of letting them know he wasn't to be messed with. Jake reminisces that if he was to 'come in crying' as a result of being picked on then his father would authorise him to 'get back out there and smack him!'

Whilst Jake never had the same experiences as his father did growing up, the 'fight to survive' mentality was evidently an inheritance passed down to Jake. However, Jake insists he never punched anyone or used violence for the sake of it, and that if he ever did resort to fisticuffs outside of the boxing ring then it was reserved exclusively for defence.

One would make the false assumption that it was around this time, with Jake progressing through his early teens and delivering the occasional knuckle pudding as a result of self-fortification, that he unearthed or was sent to a boxing gym for learnings in discipline. But one would be erroneous in such suppositions.

Whilst Jake did attend a boxing gym in Cleckheaton for a few months, receiving informal training in the sport, he didn't immediately fall for its charm, proclaiming that it was during the six week-long school holidays when his mother called him and informed him that it was time to go boxing. Jake, like most children enjoying the freedom that a summer away from school provided, preferred to stay and play with his friends, so 'packed it in' as far as boxing was concerned.

Jake's hiatus from boxing lasted until he was 21, when he migrated eastward to Bridlington to pursue his farrier studies. He says it was through not knowing anyone there and having nothing to keep him occupied or interested in his spare time that the sport of boxing re-emerged in his life.

Jake pro-actively sought out the East Side Amateur Boxing Gym in Hull, launching his training with coach Mike Dyson, rocking up to the facility unannounced and delivering the assertion, 'I just want to box!'

Jake recalls that he had six bouts in the amateur game whilst training at East Side ABC, and that this was what struck the match which lit the fire that was to spread and become the blazing inferno of his love for boxing, and ultimately his chosen metier.

Jake's transition into the paid ranks came about with great facility, with the tediousness of the amateurs acting as the catalyst for change. 'The referees [in the amateurs] were mardy old... buggers!' I sense another, far stronger profanity was on the tip of Jake's tongue... The strictness of the structure and the method of judging proved too sapping for Jake in the amateurs, and he confesses his astonishment that so many youngsters persist at this level for so long as 'it's just not enjoyable!'

The terminating component in nudging Jake in the direction of the professional side of boxing came when he obtained a cut on his eye during the novice championships. His father entered the changing room post-fight to check on Jake's wellbeing and 'this miserable old bugger followed him in, shouting "get out, only coaches are allowed in here!"' It was at this very moment that Jake was struck by the realisation that this wasn't how he wanted to be treated within the sport.

An aperture of around four years sprawled between Jake bidding 'farewell' to the amateurs and trying his fists at the pros. He was taking part in occasional white collar boxing shows; competitions designed for boxers fighting at a lower risk level, with protective gear, and matched against similar competencies. Because of the slack measure of white collar boxing, Jake wasn't training well and was on the road much of the time, fighting for a couple hundred pounds, when

Bradford-based amateur coach Peter Kennan catechized him as to why he was risking it all fighting for £200 when he could turn over (apply for a professional license), and earn a considerable amount more money for doing, what is in essence, the exact same thing.

Peter Kennan continued to prompt Jake towards turning over, but when the former English super-featherweight champion and Bradford-grounded friend of Jake's augmented this motivation, inviting him down to Dicky's Old School Gym in Batley, the taunt to turn professional was taken seriously.

When Jake retorted the beckoning, he arrived at the gym somewhere between welter and super-welterweight (147 – 154 lb), vastly exceeding the 126 lb (featherweight) limit at which he has made a name for himself fighting around Britain. He recollects that his previous manager and new gym comrades took one look at him and conveyed the jarring veracity that there was a superabundance of labour ahead and that he wouldn't be fighting for dough any time in the near future.

It was a staggering moment for Jake when he was faced with the realisation that not only had he managed to melt away the additional flesh he'd been carrying, but that he had achieved this in just a few short months, slotting comfortably into the featherweight class and re-entering talks of fighting professionally at 124 lb. Ironically Jake was informed he now needed to 'go and eat something' so as not to give away weight which might prove advantageous to any prospective opponents.

This rapid personal progression in training led to Jake's debut being arranged for 20th October 2018, where he would trade gloves with Delmar Thomas (currently inactive at the time of writing this); a fighter who went AWOL following three consecutive defeats, leaving behind a record of 5-3-0. This 'turning over' for Jake occurred just ten months after he first set foot in the professional gym, a feat worthy of note when one considers most trades and jobs take a great deal longer to learn before being 'let loose' to practice said profession.

There was a gigantic learning curve for Jake to ride, and many new things to become accustomed to in the pro ranks, such as maintaining a steady weight and not bestowing the 'whip hand' upon the likes of Delmar Thomas, as was the case in his aforementioned debut battle. The bout was set to be a super-featherweight contest, which Jake honourably reveals was 'way too heavy [to cope with]', weighing in at 133 lb, three pounds lighter than his opponent, a difference in mass that in greater divisions like light-heavy, cruiser, and heavy, would barely raise an eyebrow, but in light classes like this could be analogised to cutting off one's fighting hands.

I ask Jake how easy it is to shift between weight classes, and whether being able to do so opens up doors to more opportunities and earnings, and he warns me that whilst he has the ability to shed down to as low as 112 lb (flyweight), thus dropping four divisions, 'there is no point.' This transformation would only leave Jake devoid of energy and at a monstrous power disadvantage, escalating the risk to his health, and even life, for the same sum of money and frequency of fight offers he receives at his optimum weight. Jake quips that the only facet of tempting him to fight from such a weak position at flyweight would be a gargantuan financial offer, and even then the risk would most probably outweigh the monetary reward.

The benefaction of body load was to prove fatal on Jake's debut fight night as, to affix to the overwhelming situation of scrapping in front of a paying audience, Jake struggled to utilise his complete repertoire of tools, reasoning that he simply 'survived' and 'didn't know what to do', being adjudged the vanquished by the referee.

Jake informs me with unwavering integrity that even prior to his maiden professional ring battle he understood what his role in the sport was to be, professing, 'I knew [I would be] a journeyman.' He remembers being knocked down 'once or twice' in his scrimmage with Thomas, swiftly adopting the game plan to 'just get through.' Jake states that he wasn't hurt when he was sent to the canvas by Thomas, but that the size difference between the two contenders played a huge part. That, and the fact that it appeared obvious that Thomas had been instructed to get the fight finished early (by knockout), a design to draw attention to a winning boxer and create hype, potentially unleashing Thomas' viciousness that fateful night in Nottingham, and setting the tone for what would become a recurring theme throughout Jake's career: seeing his opponent's hand raised.

Despite hearing the final bell against Delmar Thomas, Jake wasn't so lucky in his next two bouts, as the respective referees dived in to save Jake from long-term harm before the end of the scheduled rounds against both Ismail Khan and Chris Bourke.

I quiz Jake about his feelings towards being dealt losses for each of the three fights at the initiation of his career, and whether building a losing record affected his mentality. He tells me the defeats themselves never bothered him in any way, but that owing to the fact his father shared his boxing escapades on *Facebook*, he would later have to help his family come to terms with facing questions about him losing fights, and in dealing with the negative comments so often made by 'uneducated' commentators of which boxing and social media both seem to breed in plenty.

Jake's pragmatic attitude and outlook are commendable as he willingly imparts wisdom from a sporting career which was established upon the foundations of 49 successive trounces. He shares with me that he 'just got stuck into the job', acquiring knowledge of how to ply his trade and subsist mentally with untaught fickle fans' 'strange and bizarre' views on imperfect records within the sport.

The Bradford boxer's first professional victory did not come until 1st July 2023, almost five years (1,729 days) after making the decision to 'punch for pay'. This bombshell of a result in the ring came by way of a referee's decision at York Hall, Bethnal Green, London, against Louis Smithson; an outcome Jake says 'felt no different' to when he is presented with a loss. He re-affirms how much he relishes his fights, the losses and wins alike, and compares the sensation to that of having a love for one's job where the difficult days are just a component of the overall picture, expressing, 'The decision is irrelevant, it's the fight I enjoy!'

Like in Jake's first win, he tells me he has had several fights which he feels he either won or were closer than the scores revealed. A factor that he holds accountable for such results is 'home advantage'. He re-iterates that he has and would never be expectant of a win, regardless of how well he believes he has performed, which was the rationale behind his delayed reaction when his hand was raised for the first time;

he has grown accustomed to being the loser, even when he perhaps should not have been.

Whilst many of us boxing fans have witnessed a home fighter win when, conceivably, their performance and the reaction of the spectators suggests otherwise, the topic of 'favouritism' and even corruption within boxing can be a touchy subject, and one that Jake is not overly keen to openly elaborate on. He tells me, 'I could get in trouble if I said too much!' I have read about and even heard first-hand from participants of the sport that boxers are regularly instructed not to win against chosen opponents. Not necessarily along the lines of, 'Take a dive, kid', as infamous gangster Frankie Carbo might have once enforced for betting purposes and financial gain, but more a prospect's unblemished record being shielded, where journeymen like Jake are exploited as stepping-stones for experience.

Contrary to not winning rounds on a referee or judge's score card, Jake shares with me with reputable honesty that he is acutely aware of one of the main reasons he drops points in bouts. It comes down to not throwing as many punches as his opponents do; a defence mechanism for maintaining his health and safety throughout his career. He fully appreciates that all referees and judges will have a preferred style they will score for, but tells me it can sometimes be hard to comprehend how punch output alone, and a wandering from the 'sweet science' of 'hit and don't get hit', can win a fight. When one considers the way in which a boxing match was designed to be scored, with clean shots the deciding factor in a result, Jake says it often seems that a fighter's activity, and not skill, can earn them a win. This is prevalent when Jake proclaims that 'ninety per cent of my opponents' punches are landing on my gloves or elbows', inferring that not only does work-rate trump solid defence and cleanly-landed punches, but that the objectivity of the scoring system has taken flight and subjective favouring of certain fighters has filled the void that should have been providing equality.

My respect grows exponentially for Jake throughout our conversation as he shakes off any concern for losing fights, particularly in the above manner, but exhibits admirable empathy in feeling sorry for boxers when they are taking 'their one big opportunity', and through poor refereeing and judging, it is 'stolen away from them', describing this as 'outrageous!'

I quiz Jake on what his aspirations were when he started out professionally and he pensively imagines one day being able to go home and tell his five-year-old son Roman, his world, that he has won a title of some classification. He discerns that this may never be wholly unrealistic and out of reach, but that given the type of fights he is regularly involved in (four-rounders), it would be a laborious and hazardous feat to achieve at present. It takes Jake most of the 12 minutes he is currently fighting to feel loose and warmed-up, almost peaking just as the gong calls a concluding halt to each bout, and envisages longer (six or eight rounds) fights suiting him better. Jake declares that he would bite off the hand of the person who offers him an area or English title challenge, but that his record would need to improve, albeit not dramatically.

Jake is convinced that if he began to string together a series of victories in the ring then there would be no valid reason to deny him the opportunity to fight for official honours. That being said, this could jeopardise the journeyman's entire career. He tells me, 'Getting a few wins is just not going to benefit me [now] whatsoever [as] the phone will stop ringing.'

The perils for a journeyman who commences to chase a title fantasy can manufacture a vicious cycle of winning a few fights; finding that promoters and managers distance their fighters from them through fear of risking a perfect record; a loss of income for the journeyman; then a lapse in opportunities for said journeyman to fight and gain experience in order to mount a title challenge. The journeyman can find themselves not just sprawled amid their shattered dreams and title-less, but worse, penniless. 'You just can't see many positives in trying to get a title!'

It all boils down to one thing, the desire that outweighs all others: the title or the money. It would be no mean feat to have the pride and luxury of bringing home a recognised belt for Roman, but he points out with blunt realism that his young son would sooner enjoy five holidays a year with his dad as a result of Jake's boxing earnings.

In parallel to sacrificing the opportunity to fight for acknowledged laurels in the sport of boxing, there have been numerous supplementary personal oblations Jake has had to make in order for him to pursue his career as a pugilist. A split from the mother of Roman has resulted in him living more than 80 miles away from his son, who resides in Bradford with his mum due to schooling ties. He has Roman stay with him on weekends and states that he has never and would never ask his own mother to look after Roman for the sake of just going out with friends, but has, however, been obliged to request this help if he is scheduled to box, especially when the calling comes far from home and requires him to travel great distances. He unstoppers his emotions in expressing to me that these occasions deeply pain him to no end, as weekends with little Roman are precious to him, but that he hopes and is convinced that his son will grow up to appreciate and recognise Jake's rationality: the financial reward which will ultimately benefit and improve Roman's future. Jake is certain that Roman will grow up to enjoy weekends away with him, watching his father fight and being able to spend quality time together.

The arrangement of only seeing Roman on weekends, Jake says, is a relatively new one. He went into a fight during the early months of 2024 with his brain harbouring worries and broodings over troubles in his personal life, and so was not entirely focused on his fight. This involuntary lapse in concentration was 'bloody dangerous', as he wasn't zeroed in on keeping himself safe throughout the bout, recounting this falter as 'serious business.'

Jake intimates that it is his sturdy defence in boxing which has carried him to the point he is at today, 67 fights deep in a meritoriously active career thus far, and that it is this asset which bears primary importance.

In the short, one-week interval between arranging to speak with Jake and actually doing so, he impressively manages to jostle another bout into his already-busy schedule, regardless of the debilitating flu-like virus he contracted immediately ahead of his clash with Zachary Phee. He tells me, 'It went alright... I got through', with such unceremonious humility that my esteem for him elevates to new heights. Any 'normal' person would no doubt relieve themselves of their employment duties when feeling unwell, but the fact that Jake turned up and fulfilled his commitment as staunchly is yet further evidence that the role of a journeyman is a long way from being ordinary. Imagine Canelo continuing on and honouring the scheduled date of an upcoming bout against, say, David Benavidez, when all but enervated with a virus, with his undisputed world title on the line? It would never happen. The situation would have 'postponement' written all over it; a luxury that Jake and his counterpart journeymen just aren't afforded.

The systematic scheduling of regular fights means that he also doesn't have the luxury of tailoring his preparations for specific opponents, and just 'ticking over' in the gym, keeping fit, and following standardised boxing drills is all Jake has to keep him safe and competing well. The analysing of his opposite combatants occurs in the first round of each fight. There are too numerous an amount of competitors to prepare for in Jake's absorbing boxing programme.

Jake reflects that if he was prescribed the prospect of starting over he wouldn't change much second time around, accepting that a 'butterfly effect' could occur and it was the 'silly things' he did in his youth that taught him the lessons he is now privy to. He does, however deliberate on perhaps having taken the fight game a little more seriously, not indulging in frequent drinking sessions between bouts, but that he nurses no regrets. All experiences, good and bad, formed individual paving blocks which laid the path to the 'healthy and happy' life Jake insists he now lives. 'When I'm on my deathbed, I'll have stories to tell, and that's what it's all about!'

As far as serious injuries are concerned, he explains that he's never sustained anything significant which has kept him out of the ring, or worse, unable to enjoy his life outside of the ropes, but admits he has encountered untold quotas of 'niggles'. Niggles, which would keep most championship level boxers far away from the ring and harm's way, but indeed niggles which he rarely enters his own fights free from. 'I rarely [climb onto the canvas] without an ache or pain in one part of my body or another', he jests.

In addition to governing his own fitness, Jake self-supervises his calendar of propositions to exchange blows with other boxers, but does credit trainer Mark Curley with having a valued opinion on each of his fights. He resolutely affirms that, 'If [he] gets offered a fight for twenty grand and Mark says "no"', he would heed his trainer's virtuosity.

I'm intrigued to know which of his vocations is his main earner: boxing or farriering? 'They're both [equally profitable]', but not only does boxing have his heart, the cash per minute and effort exerted betokens pugilism as immeasurably more beneficial than shoeing horses. 12 minutes trading leather brings in the same, if not more, money than an entire day smithing. He quips with a quantity of plausibility that the latter is 'fucking hard work!'

Jake's justification for why being a journeyman boxer is his preferred calling, is that he isn't obliged to sell tickets in order to make money, and can simply turn up and earn a pre-agreed fee, minus the pressure a home fighter may be faced with.

I enquire what he surmises the part of a journeyman boxer to be. A reflective duration of hush accompanies my question, before he offers up the concise yet purposeful response that, 'A journeyman is someone who's out there serving shows and giving guys experience.' He appends this statement with, 'A journeyman isn't a bad word!' I wholeheartedly concur.

What future does the journeyman have? For Jake, retirement from the sport of boxing doesn't mean disengagement from the very thing he's earned a living from and has risked it all for. He intends to utilise his expertise in acquiring his second's license, cornering and managing boxers treading the same road on which he has blistered his feet travelling.

Jake's purposeful inspiration to persist with prize fighting week in, week out, comes via the impenetrable yearning to 'do better and be a better person' for his son Roman. And notwithstanding everything boxing has given and taken from Jake, he only hopes that his son doesn't follow in his footsteps, risking his life in exchange for money.

On the significance of journeymen in boxing, Jake declares, 'They've all fought us, whoever's at the top, they've come through us!'

Gemma in training, wearing her 'Manos de Piedra' gloves – photo courtesy of Jonny Mayo

NAME	Gemma Ruegg
D.O.B	24th December 1984
BIRTHPLACE	Bournemouth, Dorset
FIGHTS OUT OF	Bournemouth, Dorset
DEBUT PRO FIGHT	22nd October 2021
FIRST WIN	22nd October 2021
FROM DEBUT TO WIN	0 days
FIGHT WEIGHT	Flyweight (112 lb)
PRO RECORD	7-10-1

CHAPTER 5
Gemma Ruegg

For the purpose of thoroughly grasping what a journeyman (in the androgynous sense) is, it would be wholly irresponsible to discount many of the factors which formulate everything a journeyman is not. Enter, Gemma Ruegg.

It is undeniably as stiffening and crystalline as a knockout win, leaving behind no confusion of who is the victor, that Gemma does not envisage herself as an undertaker of the journeyman assignment. Though brimming with admiration and esteem for all who risk their lives and livelihood in the boxing ring, Gemma insists with plausible directness that her aspirations lie within a winning record, and even potentially one which yields titles of the highest order.

But not treading the typical track of a journeyman has meant that she really has, and still is, doing things the hard way.

She explains that, unlike in the men's game, 'You don't really get journeywomen', because there just is not anywhere near the number of competitors yet, and despite the women's code having seen substantial growth over the past decade, owing in part to the exposure Katie Taylor, Chantelle Cameron, and Amanda Serrano have brought to the sport, 'Everyone [in women's boxing] is pretty much going out to win!'

Gemma's passion for boxing and her striving to achieve sizeable glory emits effortlessly as we broach the subject of her 8th September 2023 fight with Jasmina Zapotoczna. The result evidently irks her as she declares, 'What a shit decision that was! I really felt like I fucking had that one!' And as a minute fragment of the paying spectatorship, I can sincerely sympathise with her.

In a fight that, viewing live (and unofficially scoring in my head), within a Ruegg-rich atmosphere, I saw the bout as a close, yet definitive, 77-75 win for Gemma. So I, too, was astonished to witness referee Lee Every raise the Wakefield-situated Pole's arm in victory, announcing a perplexing 79-75 verdict for the 'away' fighter.

The frustration in Gemma's voice is utterly conspicuous as we agree that perhaps something ever-so-slightly sinister may have been at work where the scoring of this bout was concerned… Perhaps the fortification of a loss-less record in the away corner?

I can also discern the resolute motivation in her tone as she exclaims, 'We got the rematch!' (scheduled for June 2024).

The loss to Zapotoczna was history regurgitating on Gemma, as she had, only a matter of three weeks prior to meeting her Polish rival between the ropes, been dealt what she gleaned to be another injustice, receiving a draw for her efforts against Inna Statkevych over six rounds in Bournemouth.

The remarkable thing, when compared with some of the journeymen in these pages and unfathomable results they have endured, is that both of these losses for Gemma took place in her home town of Bournemouth, on a show by her own promoter, Steve Bendall!

There is no apparent bitterness present in her outlook, more a vexing knowledge that, in her case, as an aspiring prospect-come-champion, an accumulation of losses could prove to be time-consuming set-backs in her chase for titles.

Laurels have, in fact, been something Gemma, through both merit and perhaps a thinness in the supply of female challengers, has had the serendipity of fighting for. She went glove-to-head with Nicola Hopewell at the Magna Centre in Rotherham for the coveted Commonwealth Boxing Council flyweight championship. This was yet another example of a match in which the outcome, in the opinion of many, could have gone either way, which was ultimately adjudged a 94-97, 94-96, and 92-99 unanimous decision loss for the South Coast lady.

Rewind 33 years, and the Bournemouth-born-and-raised boxer had already begun to lay the foundations for a career in combat, regularly participating in taekwondo with her older sister. Born between two sisters, she gratefully recalls her role-model father, a 'judo phenomenon' himself, encouraging his daughters to be learned in martial arts, a discipline Gemma would uphold until around the age of 14 years.

She describes a lack of structure throughout her teenage years as being the reason for her 'life going off the rails' in these early years. A chaotic pattern of battles with mental health issues, and a complete lack of available support from professionals, tempted Gemma to wander the winding, tumultuous path of alcoholism. She openly confesses that by just 16 years old she was a registered alcoholic; a ferocious revolution of degrading wellbeing, followed by excessive booze consumption, where the drink would exacerbate her mental health unrest, tightened like a hangman's noose.

Fractious relationships with ex-partners only increased Gemma's frequency to reach for the bottle, leaving her in a world of darkness, devoid of any slither of positivity. That is, until the bright lights situated above a boxing ring slowly, but surely, melted away the edges of the blackness, and brought about a hopeful direction where, for so long, there had been an infinite chasm of nothingness.

She delineates her father as her 'best friend', and talks of her endless-valuing of working alongside him as a plumbing and heating engineer, a profession she expresses that she 'absolutely loved'. Unfortunately, a real lack of assistance for people battling the aforementioned demons meant that even strong father-daughter relationships are sometimes not enough to keep one buoyant on a troubled sea. It wasn't until Gemma eventually checked herself in to an alcohol rehabilitation facility that she finally 'got a grip'.

Once the gruelling brawl in combatting alcoholism had come to a never-fully conclusive end, the therapy she was able to access to build coping strategies for her mental health issues established success. That, and her sobriety, formed a positively potent potion in remedying her viewpoint and mentality.

Although on the up, Gemma was still quite unwell years later, and it wasn't until around the age of 27 that her doctor prescribed her some non-medical treatment for her recurring lowly state of mind, a tangible outlet: the gym. Unlike many of today's common regular exercisers, she simply could not foresee herself doing step-ups, or robotically rotating around gym equipment, thus a long-ingrained love for combat sports resurfaced in the form of physical training sessions with a boxing coach.

It can be debated that, if it was not for a life thus far plagued by insecurities, we may never have seen Gemma systematically tearing up boxing rings in worthy pursuit of belts around her waist.

In a mere matter of months, she had extirpated any medication from her recovery, and had fallen in love with the knuckled art form, immersing herself in full training and preparation for a real bout, even marrying her boxing trainer and soul-mate Danny along the way!

Her endearment with the sport led to her turning professional during the Covid pandemic, on 22nd October 2021, at the age of 37, notably acquiring her professional license with the omission of any form of amateur career. Gemma was one of the very last applicants to achieve the obtainment of a BBBofC permit in this manner.

It was through no personal fault that she leap-frogged an amateur foundation in boxing, as when the government restrictions were implemented in a frenzy of disorganisation, six of her planned amateur contests were cancelled. Gemma's dispiritedness with the lack of fight opportunities, and constant upheaval of her boxing plans, instilled a 'nothing to lose' attitude in her, and with her step-son Mace already a practising professional, she saw no negatives in following suit.

The sweet taste of victory came immediately for Gemma, ash she boxed her way to a debut 60-54 shut-out decision against Klaudia Ferenczi, with referee Kieran McCann overseeing at Central Hall, Southampton.

Contrastingly, her joy was shattered a little over a month later, as she encountered her first defeat at the gloved fists of Tysie Gallagher in Sheffield, a fighter Gemma honourably respects as having won the referee's decision 'fair and square'.

Gemma fell victim to two further successive points losses to Emma Dolan and Chloe Watson, both then, and still, undefeated (6-0-0 and 7-0-0 respectively).

As a 'baby' of the paid ranks, and now more than ever, her hankering to not just get through the rounds, but to prove herself as the better fighter in each bout, is a priority pitted leagues above that of any monetary gain. The steep but sublime learning curve, and reward of a vastly improved mental state procured by Gemma, are instances of boxing paying dividends for someone who is, outside of the prize ring also, a true fighter.

Whilst losing a fight brings with it a low, it is the continuous scheduling of bouts which keeps her on a healthy and productive trail. Failing to win, particularly under controversial circumstances, can be tremendously deflating. Regardless of a fight's outcome, the fight itself brings the buzz and addictive 'high'; a high unlike many in Gemma's past which were synthetic highs tethered to alcoholism; and one which leaves her in a contented head space.

Where a journeyman often enters a fight expecting to lose, Gemma steps into the roped arena believing she can win every single time. The corruption so frequently conspired of in boxing circles, especially where shock results occur, has never been present in Gemma's career, at least to her knowledge. She has, however, expressed surprise at some of her own results, including those in which she is absolutely certain she has won several rounds in, only to be faced with a wide-score loss.

Furthermore, she confesses that she has been privy to conversations between some of her male colleagues, where an acute awareness that they ae not supposed to win has been prevalent, and 'as long as they go out and do their jobs, they'll get paid.' By 'do their jobs', I interpreted this to connote 'give a prospect a win on their record whilst causing them little trouble.' This, in turn, would indicate that if a journeyman were to 'get above their station', the reprimand would be the costly exclusion from future paydays. Gemma not only views this perspective as a mechanical component of the sport, but an unrewarding and fruitless one too.

For her, she can afford to treat boxing as a competitive field in which to live her dreams of chasing titles, as it is not her sole money-bringer. She tells me that it would definitely impact her if she could not fight for one reason or another, and it always has to be worth her while to do so, but her trendy fitness and gym-wear company *Combat Dollies* provides a supplementary income.

On top of boxing and managing her apparel business, Gemma also trains a host of amateur boxers, and says it is of critical importance that quality time with her family is always set aside. It's fair to state that she could well use a 25-hour day!

If you have ever watched one of Gemma's fights on TV, or have been present in person, you will already know just how true the phrase 'family business' is to her where boxing is concerned. With her husband Danny in her corner, and her son Boston donning leprechaun attire and cavorting down the ramp as her mascot at the start of each fight, it is copiously clear the extent of the family's relationship with boxing, and one another, is exceptionally tight.

Gemma informs me that little Boston, approaching ten years old, is 'counting down the days' with excited anticipation until he is permitted to fight as a youth. I ask of

Gemma's concerns regarding seeing her son taking punches, and she shares that her young Hector-Camacho-esque offspring, designing his own fight-wear, has already developed a solid aptitude for ring-generalship, learning to defend and attack properly precisely *because* she has stepped back and allowed him to gain proficiency. Gemma firmly believes that if she had been 'one of those mums' and stepped in to protect her son, it would have been detrimental to his development and confidence; something she has battled with for much of her life; and does not wish her own children to suffer through.

When it comes to preparing for a bout, Gemma says Danny 'leaves no stone unturned', researching her prospective opponents to death, all in the name of ensuring his wife's readiness in the ring is at its peak; a trait and tactic much less adopted by journeymen ring-frequenters whom tend not to have this kind of time for tailoring their approach.

She tells me that her aggressive application to each fight, where she 'goes for it' and gives it her all, can be accredited to husband and trainer Danny, whom 'took every fight going and gave his opponents hell!' She adds that he, like her, has been the recipient of some 'shit decisions', and that highly-regarded ex-professional boxer Carl Greaves admitted that Danny gave him one of the hardest nights of his life in the ring.

Gemma's willingness to accept every fight offer made to her can even be regarded as in keeping with that of a journeyman, however, she indicates that the main difference between her role and theirs is that a journeyman remains, on the most part, defensive throughout, allowing them to fight much more frequently, whereas in fighting less often (up to eight times per year), she is afforded the ability to go for broke and take more risks whilst attacking.

Owing to the fact that she continues to go after titles, and refuses to put herself in the away corner as a journeyman, she remains under pressure to sell tickets to each of her fights.

After paying 'the house' (usually Steve Bendall at The O_2 Academy in Bournemouth), and covering her opponent's expenses, she has, in the past, actually lost money rather than profited from risking her life and health in the ring. She maintains this stoic stance so as to keep the opportunities of challenging for honours within her sights, rather than treat boxing as 'just a job'.

It is an immensely strenuous situation to weigh up: persevere with the pressures of ticket-selling for potential future titles, making less money, or, guaranteed regular income from fighting more often, but with the increased risk of damage through scores more punches to the head?

Gemma's situation is a unique one, where, whilst she loves the sport of boxing, she says that her 'need' for it outweighs that passion. For her to feel that 'buzz' and maintain her mental wellbeing, a fight must be an equal, fifty-fifty battle, 'not a spar', an opposing stance to that adopted by journeymen.

When all is said and done, and her body eventually disagrees with its participation in the punch-dance routine, the 'Rebel', whom 'never [does] anything by the book', will always be close to the sport. Being the proud holder of her second's license, allowing her to 'corner' other boxers, she intends to train future professional boxers, growing them from young amateurs into successful champions.

For a seemingly fearless woman who boxed in front of thousands at the O_2 Arena in London on the undercard of heavyweight superstar Anthony Joshua's clash with Robert Helenius, Gemma admits she does have one cause for trepidation: the fear of 'falling over' during her ring walk! That she exhibits no consternation for the violence of ring action itself speaks volumes for just how plucky the Bournemouth flyweight really is.

Her commitment, dedication, and unceasing work ethic to win fights, and potentially prize belts, is inherently unbending. Whether a string of victories sees a championship strap wrapped around her mid-riff, or a procession of defeats compels her to hit the road in search of regular, guaranteed work as a female journey-'man' is yet unforeseen. One thing is beyond doubt, however: her role in the sport, representing prospects and challengers alike, is another critical brick in the boxing tower, without which the entire edifice topples. Without which an entire assemblage of people do not get paid. And without which the show will not go on.

A journeyman can become a prospect, a prospect can become a champion, a champion can become a prospect, and a prospect can become a journeyman. The shift between these roles is ever-feasible and ever-fickle, and whilst it may be impossible to impose one such label to some boxers, there is a definitive distinction between the duties shouldered by each. Where ambitions alone cannot determine a boxer's status; choice, circumstance, skill, pride, and a smattering of luck may be the comprehensive ingredient list for the recipe to define oneself.

Harley after his bout with Morgan Sellamuthu – photo courtesy of Paul Emery

NAME	Harley Collison
D.O.B	10th April 1993
BIRTHPLACE	Bournemouth, Dorset
FIGHTS OUT OF	Southampton, Hampshire
DEBUT PRO FIGHT	24th June 2023
FIRST WIN	24th June 2023
FROM DEBUT TO WIN	0 days
FIGHT WEIGHT	Middleweight (160 lb)
PRO RECORD	2-1-2

CHAPTER 6
Harley Collison

Both men tap gloves in a symbol of mutual respect, entering the fourth and final round of what has been a well-fought, even matchup. Harley Collison versus Morgan Sellamuthu has drawn appreciable numbers to the O_2 Academy venue in Bournemouth, owing to both boxers residing locally, inadvertently creating a derby bout.

The referee steps back and the bell rings to prompt the action to recommence for the last time this evening. Chants and screams alternating between, 'Go on, Harley!', and, 'Come on, Morgan!', bellow out from around the upper circle of the old theatre hall in a mangled cacophony.

Collison lunges in with two piston-like left jabs to the body, with the aim of removing all wind from Sellamuthu's sails. The latter paws at Collison's leather, and in that split-second raising of Sellamuthu's arms, Collison detects the opening like a lion stalking an antelope, and delivers a right-left pair of hooks, forcing his foe to the ropes. Both sidle back into the centre of the canvas and Collison, acting quickest, immediately lets rip a series of body shots, impelling Sellamuthu to give ground again.

The proud gladiators of the modern fighting world come shoulder to shoulder, with both testing one another with traded fists to the ribs. As they break, looking each other in the eyes for a sign of weakness, Collison throws a straight right on the way out of the huddle, catching Sellamuthu on the temple. The latter replies with a left hook to Collison's head, but his target is moving backwards, so the punch has little impact.

The following twenty-or-so seconds is a display of equal exchanges, with Sellamuthu catching Collison to the jaw with a stiffening straight shot; a strike that would have shaken the most hardy of men, but did not even appear to register with Collison.

Collison turns his opponent and manhandles him back to the ropes, receiving two more accurate thwacks to the face in the process; again, barely rippling the former's features.

Collison eludes Sellamuthu's defensive stance and sneaks two jarring uppercuts to the chin of his opponent. All the while, chants of 'finish him!' ring out expectantly from those there in support of Collison. Is this a sign of awareness from his backers that a knockout may be required in order to guarantee victory as the away fighter?

Collison unleashes a gloved assault like a man possessed, exerting every joule of energy in this final stanza war, landing on Sellamuthu's jaw and glancing leather off the top of his head.

There is no let-up as Sellamuthu feels the ropes imprinting on his spine yet again, pinned by an onslaught of Collison combinations. Sellamuthu's reserves are sapping rapidly as he pushes the full mass of his aggressor backwards after each barrage, only to see Collison stride right back inside for his preferred intimate phone box scrap.

Collison's output steps up to a gear previously unknown. Sellamuthu is scoring on occasions, but the flesh wall in front of him is unmoving.

Sellamuthu's fans roar as a one-two breaks through to Collison's face, but are immediately silenced as the latter instantly steams forward again. The seconds tick in seemingly slow motion as a slug-fest ensues; that not unfamiliar to historical greats like Jack Dempsey, Joe Louis, and Rocky Marciano.

Neither quits punching until the concluding bell, a ring over-extended so as to ensure both men hear it and stop trading knuckles. Exhausted, and with the utmost respect, the pair clasp, then proceed to parade around with their arms raised in perceived victory. A victory, after four long, thoroughly entertaining rounds, I feel sure belongs to Collison.

Whilst judging and scoring differs from person to person, and a substantial amount of subjectivity plays a part in boxing match results, home fighter preferential treatment also appears prevalent from card to card.

The ring MC takes up the microphone and announces, 'After four scintillating rounds of boxing, your referee, Mr Shaw, scores this fight thirty-nine to thirty-seven', with the referee simultaneously raising Sellamuthu's gloved fist and inflicting Collison's first professional defeat, in only the latter's third bout. A defeat he would later tell me he does not agree with, but holds no contempt for, saying, 'That's just the game.'

****

In the small council house-flecked suburb of Pennington, The New Forest, a seven year-old, angelic-featured boy runs timidly around on the misshapen, lumpy green, a central feature bounded by parked cars, as an estate-wide free-for-all football match takes place. The boy, it seems, would be effortlessly unbalanced and overturned by a stiff breeze. The young boy's family life is a happy and full one, with the perfect mix of discipline and freedom to provide the platform for him to achieve whatever he sets his mind to.

****

Stereo-typically, a boxer is the product of a perturbed childhood. So how did it come to be that the innocent, polite, even shy, young Harley Collison transfigured into the stern-faced, clout-bringing, stocky middleweight glove-swinger, slipping a metaphorical middle finger to the human meat conveyor belt 'system' of modern professional boxing, that he is today?

From his accouchement, Harley was raised in Bournemouth by his mother Lin, and father Paul, until the city's seedier side became tiresome for them. With concern for raising their children in an area where neighbouring households were dealing drugs, and other petty crime plagued local youthhood, Lin and Paul secured a relocation to a council property in Pennington, which they quickly purchased and recast into a stylish contemporary home, adorned by an exotic garden of palms and Mediterranean flora. I can remember vividly being terrified to touch anything in their house, even the toilet flush of their nautical themed first-floor bathroom; not through fear of being told off, but owing to the fact the house was proudly immaculate!

The middle of a sibling batch of three; one older sister, one younger sister, Harley's family life was a sanguine experience, where he was given an interminable leash to go out and explore unaccompanied... So long as he watched his 'Ps and Qs' when he returned home.

He proclaims that he 'had nothing to complain about' where his childhood was concerned, but was struck with the realisation at 16 years old, that it was time to flee the nest, a non-negotiable ultimatum, and one which was expected.

Harley followed in the footsteps of his father, becoming 'a man' and going solo in the world as soon as he left school, making the bold move 20 miles from home to Bedford Place in Southampton; an urban locality teeming with student life, and rich in watering holes to cater for all dispositions.

Rather than implode under the pressure of youthful independence, Harley had a 'brilliant time' initially, studying at college in Eastleigh for a short while. Nevertheless, the obligation to support himself on £130 per week swiftly brought attention to the fact that a supplementary income was necessary. As with so many young people struggling financially in Britain, some of the common, undisclosed-by-Harley, issues arose in his life.

In order to relieve some of the stress caused by growingly difficult self-ruling, he started 'pumping weights', which had an immediate positive impact on his state of mind. But this was not quite sufficient in lifting him above the parapet, so a pot-shot calling upon Jack Bishop's gym in Southampton materialised, and thus, an extensive and revealing relationship with boxing was set in motion.

Harley had only been attending the boxing gym for around two months when he felt that he had naturally absorbed the methodology of the sport, and so sought out a 'proper' fight on an unlicensed show. He triumphed in this bout and caught the fistic bug, progressing into amateur competitions with barely a breath inhaled between the two, before back-tracking to the white collar circuit and building a record of thirteen consecutive unbeaten results.

Despite this novel endorphin-releasing venture, stability in his life had all but evanesced, with wild weekends 'on the piss', and impulsively extensive travels around South-East Asia occupying tremendous portions of this period in his life.

Upon returning from his exploits abroad, Harley launched himself into The Queensbury League, and found the limelight through a succession of pugnacious performances in the ring, scalping popular Max Chart along the way to win the national light-heavyweight strap.

There was never a design for his transition from the vested ranks to the paid game, but his recognition that he could perhaps 'be more than just alright' at boxing, coupled with his close-knit boxing fraternity urging that he 'had nothing to lose', affirmed his decision to take the leap to the licensed version of the trade.

In the wake of 21 combined unlicensed and amateur bouts, and nine years of collusion with boxing, Harley forked out £1,000 to obtain his paperwork from the BBBofC, but was harshly rebutted due to his relative inexperience, and lack of amateur pedigree, which could pose a significant risk in a version of the sport where head guards are reserved only for sparring.

This minor set-back was expeditiously overcome, as Harley boxed in the amateurs for a further half-season (six months), which proved to be acceptable in the in the view of the Board, seeing his second application for a professional license granted.

His introductory pro bout, and first brush with a boxer he would describe as a 'journeyman', came in the form of Italian light-heavyweight, Southwark-based Victor Edagha; a fighter whose record at the time was 2-79-3. He recounts the fight as being an 'awkward' introduction into the paid ranks, as his opponent was 'clearly not there to win', throwing sparingly; something Harley found bemusing to wrap his mind around. Despite having to take the fight to Edagha, and being aware that the Londoner's pessimistic style was making his own game look less than fetching, he was deservedly awarded a shutout 40-36 decision by referee Sean McAvoy.

This first victory as a pro 'got the ball rolling', but against a man who covered up for much of the contest, Harley takes no pride or glory from the manner in which he succeeded. His ambition is to be able to give a hundred per cent in every bout against opposition whom reciprocate the labour and, win or lose, he can rest satisfied.

The opportunity soon arose, in September 2023, for Harley to project his name in a fight which he sensed would be a real fifty-fifty battle. This was set for Bethnal Green's York Hall, going toe-to-toe with Essex-based Scotsman Danny Boyle, whose unvanquished record remains intact as of the time of writing this (3-0-1).

Incidentally, the sole mild blemish on Boyle's record is a respectable draw, an inseparable deadlock in the eyes of Kieran McCann, and one which came at the resolution of the hard-fought skirmish with Harley. Watching the fight live at the old East End boxing venue, I would concur that a tie is a fair reward for the endeavours of both fighters, however, at the time, I leant slightly towards a winning score for Harley.

The third of his fights came in the guise of the aforementioned controversial loss to Morgan Sellamuthu, a result he says 'hasn't been eating [him] up', but one which, after re-watching it countless times, he cannot comprehend the scoring of three rounds to one in favour of the opposite corner.

In the three months that superseded, from February to May 2024, an array of derailing circumstances led to Harley arrogating an alternate character, donning the interim mask of a 'social media boxer'. From opponents pulling out at the eleventh hour, to planned competitors dictating mouth-watering fees of £500 per round from his own pocket, aggrandised by his yearning to not fight journeymen for an 'easy win', Harley was backed into a corner. Expressing heightened agitation at a lapse in ring activity, he took to *Instagram* to call out Sellamuthu to 'run it back'.

Both Sellamuthu's and Harley's organised adversaries had evaded capture and peeled away from promoter Steve Bendall's 'Havoc in Hamble' card in April, paving the way for a rematch between the two, and the chance to settle the score.

It appeared that Harley posed too big a risk for Sellamuthu as the former's approach was rebuffed without hesitation. Sellamuthu's *Instagram* story aired his video response to Harley's beckoning, declaring, 'You were a good stepping stone… Stay in your lane!' Sellamuthu went on to confidently claim, 'I beat you fair and square in September [2023]!' One thing is utterly limpid where this rivalry is concerned: there is unfinished business to be resolved!

This entire public exchange, Harley confesses, is atypical of his behaviour and personality, but was a building culmination of vexations propelling him to try a new tack in getting the fights he so desperately seeks.

Harley's two victories came against men he would label as conventional journeymen, and believes that because his record is balanced, with two wins, one loss, and two draws, that prospective opponents have already begun to steer well clear of the threat he poses. He adds, 'Anyone who knows anything about boxing will look at my two draws and think,

"He probably won those"', and so fighters with winning records, or prospects starting out in the sport, are likely to circumnavigate the Southampton punch-painter. This has left him in an intolerable state of affairs, where he feels compelled to reject fight offers from journeymen which will 'prove nothing' to him, but also despairingly short of invitations to fight in genuine even-level bouts.

When I was first re-acquainted with Harley, following almost a two-decade hiatus, he conceded to me, 'I'll probably end up being a journeyman.' However, since his move to the House of Pain gym, under the masterful tuition and management of Danny Ruegg, a man whom Harley says he trusts implicitly, a transformation of thought process has transpired.

He shares with me that Danny's gym instils a 'do or die' mentality in a 'dog eat dog' environment, where head gear is non-existent, and a rough 'n' tough scrapper like Harley can flourish. He expresses the utmost respect for the job in which a journeyman devotes themselves to, acknowledging that there is serious money to be earned without the pressure of selling tickets, but 'swallowing [his] ego' is something that, upon recent reflection, he is not prepared to do. Yet.

Taking part in bouts against journeymen is something that Harley says he doesn't have time for, and at 31 years old, an age at which many boxers would consider themselves to be past their prime, the 'warm-up' vibe in these fights is a notion he had hoped he'd left behind in the amateurs. Losing is not the issue, he assures me, especially if he is beaten whilst 'showing heart' in a memorable ring war, but the mechanism of being paid to lose is an arrangement Harley discerns he would not 'look back and feel proud of.'

He tells me that even the slightest portrayal of toughness, be it a video of him dragging truck tires through wet mud for strength training, in a Balboa-esque manner, can be enough to deprive him of work. Again, Harley imputes this to rival boxers in-the-know, whom hope to achieve something in the sport, viewing him as a threat and fancying no involvement with someone in such condition.

He admits that he could very easily fork out thousands of pounds from his own pocket over the next year, paying journeymen to lose against him and 'pad' his record, but shrugs 'what's the point?' He is adamant that even if he boosted his record with six wins against journeymen, he would gain absolutely no 'buzz', and would lose money in the process, but more importantly to him, he would learn nothing about himself and not develop one iota.

Harley candidly divulges to me that he fully appreciates the reasons why a journeyman adopts said role, as he himself has been in financial crises in the past, living nomadically in his converted van with his two German Shepherds, waking up in a different location every morning. Yet the pressure of selling tickets and breaking even at best, just to fight a worthy opponent whom provides a test and challenge, is still not enough for him to swallow his pride and opt for the regular income that being a journeyman would provide. He reveals that it would be exceptionally onerous for him to accept a mountain of losses 'just for money', in fights he knows that, without a 'system of control' dictating the success of certain boxers, he is sure he would otherwise win.

Whilst the sport of boxing 'saved' his physical being in many ways, Harley believes that if he was to 'give in' and travel the journeyman's path before really 'giving it a go' and challenging for titles, then his pride and legacy would be greatly impacted.

Harley finds himself at a crossroads of sorts, where one road, the left-hand prong takes him on a one-way peregrination to *Journeymanville*; a gun-slingers' town where there are financial spoils and regular shoot-outs aplenty, if he is willing to trade in his ambitions. The middle prong leads him to *Prospectborough*; a fashionable up-and-coming city, where it's each for their own, and despite the glittering belts dangling tantalisingly on the horizon, just out of reach, and the evenly-matched fights he keenly pursues, one slip-up could U-turn his vehicle and send him careering homewards. And the third and final, right-hand prong of the fork, a far-dustier and less forgiving terrain leads him to *Bareknuckleton*; a gladiator-like coliseum of glory in which to supplant his name eternally in this 'underworld', but a place which, akin to Roman times, poses significant danger to his life and offers no guarantee of riches.

An impending brain scan due in June 2024 could ram Harley into the bare-knuckle, unlicensed side of the sport if a clean bill of health is not issued; something he has already accepted and is prepared for. But just one 'good' win against a notable opponent in the gloved code could secure him his much-anticipated return with Morgan Sellamuthu for the Southern Area strap. However, a journeyman is something he 'will not be forced to become.' If it happens, he attests, then it will be on his own terms.

In the very same way that the Parkstone luminary Freddie Mills elevated himself from fairground booth brawler to world light-heavyweight champion in 1948, the durable English Oak that is Harley Collison is on a journey of his own; to prove himself... To himself!

EPILOGUE

I'll ask again, *what is a 'journeyman' boxer?*

As previously mentioned, approximately 1,100 boxers currently holding licenses to fight professionally in Britain traipse the country regularly throughout the year, eagerly answering the call for 'work'. Many of these grafters will never be gifted the opportunity to fight on pay-per-view shows or at major stadiums like Wembley, on cards amongst the stars of the sport, with the incentive of changing their lives financially in a matter of 47 minutes or less, and will trundle on resiliently, fighting around the 'small hall circuit'.

The iconic York Hall in Bethnal Green, London, is one such small hall venue, providing space for circa 1,250 spectators, continuing the traditions and atmospheres of historical halls long gone from across London; halls like The Ring in Blackfriars; Wonderland in the East End; or even Premierland on Back Church Lane. Whilst it will be the fantasy of most contemporary professional boxers to battle beneath the great lights of stadia, it must be stated that many of the most highly-regarded British fights I have seen, heard and read about have taken place in venues like York Hall, Bournemouth O_2 Academy, Memorial Grounds (East London), and Mountbatten Centre in Portsmouth.

These small hall productions tend to be the fundamental building blocks for boxers turning over and harbouring hopes to assemble a record worthy not just of being noticed, but also capturing the financial backing of a major player in the promotional game; say, a Mr Edward Hearn, or a Mr Francis Warren.

For those lucky enough to be on the 'right' end of results, constructing win upon win through the early bouts in their career, be it through 'home' fighter treatment, skilled points victories, or even the indisputable conclusion of a knockout, only then will a fighter generally be considered a 'prospect'.

A prospect boxer will customarily persevere with bearing the cargo-like burden of having to sell tickets in order to earn money from fighting, but will likely be blessed with easier fights, and therefore wins, amounting to a 'padded' but much more marketable record; more importantly, a record containing no losses. This trade-off will continue to be a prosperous, two-way street for boxer and promoter, providing the latter's pockets are kept fatly lined with paper containing the late-Queen's image.

And for those fighters unable to establish a loyal following willing to constantly shell out their hard-earned cash, rendering it nigh on impossible to sell all of the tickets allocated to them by the promoter? And those who have found themselves on the 'wrong' end of one too many decisions as the 'away' fighter? Often these turn out to be the very subject matter of this book: journeymen.

A journeyman may benefit from shirking the responsibility of selling tickets, with many getting paid either a lump sum to 'just turn up', or per round completed. Most of the boxers I have spoken with would play it safe and agree to a lump sum of, say, £600-£1,500 for a four, six or eight round fight, rather than accepting the more lucrative but risky offer of £300-£500 per round completed. But then again, several of the boxers featured in this book find themselves encumbered by the necessity to sell tickets in order to make money for themselves, and so diverting focus from their training and home lives to toiling their phone contacts lists and rallying their friends and families on numerous instances throughout the year. It's also of requisite significance to moot the point that if one of the aforementioned 'journeymen' strays back towards their dreams and goals, and starts to win bouts, they may very well find themselves out of the job, with payday frequencies decreasing dramatically when other fighters and managers see them as a dangerous fighter posing a risk to unbeaten records. This can then knock on to the boxer being unable to secure meaningful experience in the ring, and therefore without a path of their own to follow. They become a 'journeyman in limbo', if you will.

One of the recurring themes and a common misconception of journeymen is that these men and women, many of whom rack up over 100 fights in their careers, losing the vast majority of them, are in fact no good at boxing. As a frequent attendee of small hall boxing shows I can absolutely and unequivocally counter the above dissension and vouch that nearly every journeyman boxer I have seen fight, particularly and especially those within the pages of this book, will be offered fights and asked back to contest within this sport precisely because they *are* skilled and reliable in their trade.

One of the main duties of a journeyman includes being available at short notice to rescue a bill on which a fighter may have pulled out, either through injury or otherwise, and so fitness and keeping their 'tools' sharp is of the utmost importance.

Many journeymen rely on their boxing income as their main or sole source of finance, fighting for sums as much as, or in excess of, £1,500 fortnightly, and so avoiding damage and injury is unreservedly critical to their livelihood. This only highlights further just how skilled a journeyman must be if one is to register 29 fights in a year, as Dale Arrowsmith accomplished throughout 2023.

More often than not a journeyman never intends to lose, principally at the dawning of their professional career, but when a steady inward flow of cash is presented, along with the guarantee of regular work, garnished with the sure support and respect from anyone who knows anything about boxing, being a journeyman can, and clearly does, become a very lucrative, satisfying, and fulfilling alternative to fighting once or twice a year and protecting one's record in the hopes of attaining a championship title, all the while carrying the probable perils and downfalls that one blemish to a record would bring.

I can only venture a guess that if *Compubox* were to tally up the volume of punches the average journeyman takes over a year in comparison to a championship level boxer, the contrast would be astonishing! Take, for example, the year 2023. If we scan over the number of fights the highest-ranked competitor in each recognised division of *The Ring*'s rankings was involved in, and place this list alongside that of the six boxers featured in this book, the averages are worlds apart. The champions' and number one contenders' total bouts for the annum in question were: Oleksandr Usyk (1), Jai Opetaia (2), Dmitry Bivol (1), Canelo Álverez (2), Janibek Alimkhanuly (2), Jermell Charlo (1), Terence Crawford (1), Teofimo Lopez (1), Vasiliy Lomachenko (1), Emanuel Navarrete (3), Leigh Wood (3), Naoya Inoue (2), Jason Moloney (1), Juan Francisco Estrada (0), Jesse Rodriguez (2), Kenshiro Teraji (2), and Knockout CP Freshmart (0). Now take the total number of ring battles that our six journeymen-prospects fought in 2023: Dale Arrowsmith (29), Matt Hall

(20), Jordan Grannum (27), Jake Pollard (18), Gemma Ruegg (6), and Harley Collison (4). The champions' total average fights for 2023 were just over one (1.4), whilst collectively the journeymen and prospects fought a staggering average of 17 (17.3) times! These shocking statistics convey to a greater extent the risk that journeymen face on a far more mammoth frequency to those with the might of a wealthy promoter and some governing bodies behind them.

These risks range from so-called superficial injuries such as broken bones, cuts and burst ear drums, to a far more harrowing truth. The long-term effects of boxing have long been known to those involved in the sport, and punches received by a boxer, generally speaking, only exacerbate the development of Dementia Pugilistica, or boxer's dementia, or even death by CTE (Chronic Traumatic Encephalopathy), or a subdural haematoma (bleed on the brain), caused by repeated head injuries. Whilst one punch can effectively lead to any of the above ailments and tragedies at any one moment, it is a fact: the more punches one takes, the greater the chance of it happening to them.

The chief learning I have been rewarded with through engaging with the boxers in this book is that this sport gives so much to so many people from all walks of life, and even more to those willing to give their lives in return. The word 'legacy' rings loud in my ears and in decades to come all of these boxers will find their names chiselled into the eternal tomes of this sport's rich history.

All one must do is pick up any of the weekly instalments of *Boxing News*, on any given week, and the names Dale Arrowsmith, Matt Hall, Jordan Grannum, Jake Pollard, Gemma Ruegg, and Harley Collison will routinely adorn those pages, constituting hard work, grit, determination, and an overwhelming abundance of mental toughness.

They have shown themselves to be the very pillars holding this sport up, without whom there would be no 'world' champions, no wealthy promoters in their swanky condos, no shows week-in, week-out, no corner teams or managers growing rich from the busted knuckles of others, not even any fans! If champions are the hour hands, then journeymen are second hands, keeping the whole mechanism ticking.

Journeymen need boxing to make a living, but if boxing is to survive, the sport will be perpetually indebted to and in desperate need of its true heroes: journeymen.

SOURCES

Books:

- Bell, L., 1950. *Men Behind the Gloves*. 2nd edn. London: C. & J. Temple Limited.

- Bell, L., 1961. *Bella of Blackfriars*. 1st edn. London: Odhams Press Limited.

- Carvill, P., 2024. *Death of a Boxer*. 1st edn. London: Biteback Publishing Ltd.

- Giudice, C., 2020. *Macho Time*. 1st edn. Massachusetts: Hamilcar Publications.

- Harding, J., 1994. *Lonsdale's Belt*. 1st edn. London: Robson's Books Ltd.

- McRae, D., 2005. *Dark Trade: Lost in Boxing*. 3rd edn. Edinburgh: Mainstream Publishing Company Ltd.

- Mitchell, K., 2009. *Jacobs Beach: The Mob, the Garden & the Golden Age of Boxing*. 1st edn. London: Yellow Jersey.

- Odd, G. E., 1948. *Ring Battles of the Century*. 1st edn. London: Nicholson & Watson.

- Pacheco, F., 2000. *The 12 Greatest Rounds of Boxing: The Untold Stories*. 1st edn. New York: Total Sports Illustrated.

- Stanton, M., 2018. *Unbeaten: The Triumphs and Tragedies of Rocky Marciano*. 2nd edn. London: Pan Books.

- Turley, M., 2014. *Journeymen: The Other Side of the Business – A New Perspective on the Noble Art*. 1st edn. Worthing: Pitch Publishing.

- Worsell, E., 2017. *Dog Rounds: Death and Life in the Boxing Ring*. 1st edn. London: Blink Publishing.

Websites:

- *www.bbbofc.com*
- *www.boxing-fandom.com*
- *www.boxing-social.com*
- *www.boxingforum.com*
- *www.boxingnews24.com*
- *www.boxrec.com*
- *www.englandboxing.org*
- *www.islingtongazette.co.uk*
- *www.manchestereveningnews.co.uk*
- *www.maverickstarstrust.co.uk*
- *www.readersdigest.co.uk*
- *www.ringtv.com*
- *www.tapology.com*

Other sources:

- *Boxing News* (various issues dating April 2023 – June 2024).

ACKNOWLEDGEMENTS

Firstly, my endless thanks go out to the six motifs for this book, without whom my subject matter would have been scant. To Dale, Matt, Jordan, Jake, Gemma, and Harley, you have my gratitude for the time each of you gave me, and for opening up your clandestine lives and pasts to me.

Secondly, I'd like to thank Paul Emery, not only for providing me with a phenomenal collection of encapsulating boxing photos, one of which became the front cover for this book, but also for the unexpected, yet riveting, debate we had on the current state of boxing and its effects on aspiring boxers.

Next I give my appreciation to Michael Ault and Jonny Mayo, who also allowed me to include their photos of Matt and Gemma, respectively, bringing life to my text.

Finally, to Tara, Reuben, and Harper; my wife and kids; for weathering the storm whilst I spent hours, weeks, and months putting this all together after years of obsessing over boxing and verbally punching their ears off at the dinner table about the sport and this book.

Journeymen, from left to right: Matt Hall, Dale Arrowsmith, and Jordan Grannum, ahead of their respective bouts on the same card at York Hall, Bethnal Green on 1st June 2024 – photo courtesy of Dale Arrowsmith

Printed in Great Britain
by Amazon